WHAT PEOPLE ARE SAYING...

"Remember that enlivening conversation you had in line at the coffee shop or that moment of deep connection with your fellow passenger on a bumpy flight? Moments like these can alter our lives forever, if we let them. Karl Wiegers's new book, *Pearls from Sand*, beautifully and accurately captures the importance of our profound human connections, while providing lessons in nurturing and developing extraordinary relationships as an access to living life to its fullest."

Kristen Moeller, MS, bestselling author of
Waiting for Jack: Confessions of a Self-Help Junkie —
How to Stop Waiting and Start Living Your Life
www.waitingforjack.com

"In *Pearls from Sand*, Karl Wiegers shares powerful life lessons that will help you have a more fulfilling life. You'll find the true-life experiences in *Pearls from Sand* thought-provoking, insightful, entertaining, and useful."

Elizabeth Lombardo, PhD, author of the bestselling book
A Happy You: Your Ultimate Prescription for Happiness
www.AHappyYou.com

PEARLS
from SAND

How SMALL Encounters
Lead *to* POWERFUL Lessons

KARL WIEGERS

NEW YORK

PEARLS *from* SAND

How SMALL Encounters Lead *to* POWERFUL Lessons

BY KARL WIEGERS

© 2011 Karl Wiegers. All rights reserved.

ISBN 978-1-60037-999-4 Paperback
ISBN 978-1-61448-021-1 EBook

Library of Congress Control Number: 2011927219

Published by:

MORGAN JAMES PUBLISHING
The Entrepreneurial Publisher
5 Penn Plaza, 23rd Floor
New York City, New York 10001
(212) 655-5470 Office
(516) 908-4496 Fax
www.MorganJamesPublishing.com

Cover Design by:
Rachel Lopez
rachel@r2cdesign.com

Interior Design by:
Bonnie Bushman
bbushman@bresnan.net

To Chris, times seven

ACKNOWLEDGMENTS

I'm grateful to the many people who taught me the lessons I describe in this book. Some were family members: my wife, Chris; my parents, Bud and Ruth Wiegers; my siblings, Bruce Wiegers and Kathy Reynolds; and my uncle Carlin Counsell. Other mentors were teachers, particularly the late Dr. Stanley G. Smith. I learned a lot from some friends and professional colleagues over the years: Dr. Ruth Chabay, Larry Constantine, Dr. Tony Gallo, Dr. J. Arthur Gleiner, Norm Kerth, Dr. Terry Lewis, Dr. Susan Ristow, Mike and Kathy Terrillion, Mick and Diann Williams, and others. I won't name the individuals from whom I learned lessons by negative examples, but those messages were no less significant.

I appreciate the many helpful review comments I received on the manuscript from Dawn Bookert, Sal Cambareri, Norm Kerth, Linda Lewis, Lea Loiselle, Matt McDaniel, Kathy Reynolds, Holly Sander, David Standerford, Bill Trosky, and Ruth Wiegers. Thriller writer Lior Samson provided much useful input regarding publication avenues, as did Microsoft Press publisher Ben Ryan and author and screenwriter Megan Clare Johnson. I appreciate literary agent Kristina Holmes recommending Morgan James Publishing to me.

PEARLS *from* SAND

Many thanks to Barbara Hanscome and to Charity Heller and Nancy D'Inzillo of The Mighty Pen for their sharp eyes, sharp pencils, and the perfect editing touch. No matter how fine a writer you think you are, a good editor will make you look better. I'm grateful to David Hancock and the production team at Morgan James Publishing for turning the manuscript into the final product.

CONTENTS

INTRODUCTION

As we go through life, we encounter a vast array of learning experiences. We go to school, learn to read and speak and write, and perhaps learn to play a musical instrument or a sport. We pick up knowledge—and a lot of opinions—from a variety of sources: from friends, teachers, and coworkers; from books and magazines; from the Internet and television; perhaps even from strangers we meet. All of this information goes into the repository of wisdom and experience that shapes our personalities, values, behaviors, and worldview.

At various times in your life you've no doubt encountered certain teachers, relatives, and friends who influenced you. If you're paying attention, you'll observe that some of your interactions with these people contain powerful messages that stick with you for the rest of your life. Such "pearls of wisdom" often emerge from small, everyday conversations and experiences, just as a real pearl can develop from the stimulus of a tiny grain of sand inside an oyster.*

I've been fortunate to have experienced a variety of such seminal encounters in my life. Often, just a single sentence that I heard from

---

* Actually, natural pearls generally form when the oyster coats an invasive parasite, a bit of mantle, or another irritant—not a grain of sand—with nacre, but *Pearls from Parasites* didn't seem like a good title for a book.

someone really opened my eyes and changed my behavior or thinking in a constructive way. I remember those moments with crystal clarity, down to the tone of the person's voice and the expression on his or her face. Rarely does a day go by when I don't think of one or another of these powerful insights and rely on them to help guide my actions.

To my surprise, when I asked some of the people mentioned in this book if I could share the lessons I learned from them, none remembered the discussion to which I referred. These messages have made me happier and a better person, but to the other people involved it was just another random conversation with a friend, colleague, or student. You, too, might have imparted valuable life lessons to people around you without even knowing it.

Each chapter in this book describes one such life lesson that has strongly affected me, along with the conversations or other experiences that revealed the pearl of wisdom and helped me understand and apply it. I have grouped the thirty-seven lessons in this book into six parts. Part 1 describes six "interpersonal pearls" that have helped guide my interactions with other people. Eight "personal pearls" appear in Part 2; they describe experiences that taught me something important about myself or my own behavior. The six "inspirational pearls" in Part 3 relate insights from role models whose positive behaviors helped shape my values. Part 4 features five "practical pearls" with pragmatic messages that can be useful to anyone in his or her daily life. Five "cautionary pearls" appear in Part 5 with warnings about certain dangers that lurk in the world and how to detect and avoid them. Finally, Part 6 presents seven "professional pearls" that I learned in various workplaces and which can be applied to almost any work environment.

While I deduced some of these lessons on my own, through personal experience and observation, others came from professors I respected, colleagues in the software development profession, my parents and other relatives, close friends, and fellow students. By sharing my observations— along with practical suggestions about how you might apply the lessons to your own life—I hope to serve as one of those useful mentors for you. All of the anecdotes I relate in this book are true, although some names and other details have been changed to preserve privacy.

So that you understand where I'm coming from and how I came to collect this particular set of lessons and insights, I'll provide a brief biography. My father, Bud Wiegers, spent the first half of his career in the United States Air Force, and as a result, my family moved around a lot. I was born in Japan in 1953 and lived in California, Texas, Maine, Iowa, Italy, France, and Idaho before I started eighth grade, when my father retired from the Air Force. Moving around so much provides a child with many interesting experiences but not with much in the way of family or community roots. I rarely saw my grandparents or cousins, and I have kept in touch with virtually no friends from the first nineteen years of my life.

I attended high school in Boise, Idaho, and received a bachelor's degree in chemistry from Boise State College in 1973. I attended graduate school at the University of Illinois at Urbana-Champaign, where I received a master of science and a doctorate in organic chemistry. Following a year as a visiting assistant professor and a year of postdoctoral research at the University of Illinois, I went to work as a photographic research scientist at Eastman Kodak Company in Rochester, New York.

To my disappointment, my research work at Kodak wasn't much like the organic chemistry I found so fascinating. I had always enjoyed computer programming, so I transitioned into the field of software development a few years later. During the next fourteen years, I worked for Kodak as a software developer, manager, and quality engineer, eventually specializing in software process improvement. I left Kodak early in 1998 after launching my own one-person software development training and consulting company, Process Impact (Processimpact.com). I have written six books and many articles on aspects of software, management, chemistry, and military history (an interest that came from growing up on air force bases).

My life has led me through a series of activities and people that imparted certain perspectives and values. I offer this collection with the hope that you will find these pearls of wisdom relevant to your life. Even if you can't relate to the specific experiences I describe, look for the lessons that came out of them and consider how you might apply those to yourself in some way.

I also encourage you to scour your own memory for significant insights that you can pass on to your children, students, friends, or coworkers. Everyone can benefit from people who teach those around them powerful life lessons. At Pearlsfromsand.com you can read more life lessons and even share your own pearls of wisdom with the rest of the world. The pearls are all around us, if we only notice, listen, and think about them.

Part 1

INTERPERSONAL PEARLS

The chapters in this section describe lessons I've learned that helped me improve the nature and quality of my interactions with other people in various situations. In some cases, I didn't learn these lessons as early as I would have liked. Instead, I had to acquire the essential knowledge over time, often by getting it wrong at first, but then eventually learning how to get it right. It's okay to do things wrong. What's not okay is failing to notice that your initial actions weren't the best choice and repeating them, possibly leaving a string of damaged relationships in your wake.

I reflect on these pearls of wisdom nearly every day, and I try to use them to guide my behaviors and thought patterns. These lessons have helped me live a more fulfilling life than I might have had otherwise and to interact with the people around me in a more constructive way. I'm grateful to the wise friends and family members who communicated their insights to me.

Chapter 1

SECOND TIME'S THE CHARM

Pearl #1: Everyone deserves a second
chance to make a first impression.

*M*y first date with my wife, Chris, did not go well. It was entirely my fault and I make no excuses. The details are not important; suffice it to say, I was not in a good state of mind. I was distracted by thoughts of the woman who had just broken up with me instead of focusing on my date, as I should have been, even though Chris was much more my type.

I'd known Chris for several years at Kodak. She was a secretary in the research labs' training department, and we had worked together frequently on computer training projects. We had joked around with each other and even flirted a bit. I thought she was cute and funny, so I asked her out. But I wasn't good company that night. We watched a supremely boring movie, and neither of us had much fun. I felt bad afterward because I knew I hadn't properly responded to Chris's cheerful and friendly behavior, despite my attraction to her.

A couple of months passed. I was in a much better mood. One afternoon I stopped by Chris's office and excitedly told her about my new Honda Accord, which I had just picked up from the dealer. I inquired what she was doing that fine Friday evening. "Oh, just the usual," she replied. On the spur of the moment, I asked her if she wanted to go to a movie with me that night in my new car. She promptly said yes. Later, though, she told me that between then and the time I picked her up a few hours later, she had been horrified at what she had to face: another dreadful date with Karl. As it happened, we had a really good time that night. We've been having a good time for twenty-five years now.

There was a message in this experience for both of us: Give people more than one chance. In this case, I was just lucky that Chris agreed to go out with me a second time without thinking about it. Given a few moments to reflect on our previous date, she would have said no and we both would have missed out on a happy life together. They say you never get a second chance to make a first impression. But based on our experience, you might want to forget about a less-than-favorable first impression and give that person another shot.

Someone might rub you the wrong way for a number of reasons. You know nothing about how that person feels at that moment, what's going on in her life, or what might be distracting her. She might be tired or have a headache. Perhaps she has a sick child at home or has been getting grief from her boss. You might bear a physical resemblance to someone she used to know that she didn't like. She could simply be in a lousy mood. You just don't know. So if the two of you don't click, it might be worth taking advantage of a second opportunity to connect and see how it works out.

The importance of this message was reinforced another time someone gave me a second chance. I once attended a meeting with some people who worked in Kodak's information technology area, including one fellow I had never met before, an Australian bloke named Ian. I had been experiencing a lot of computer problems, and I wasn't happy about it. The man who was running the meeting and I never did get along. That day he had a particularly bad attitude and wasn't being very cooperative. (He'd probably say the same about me.) We argued about my computer issues for a few minutes. When it became clear that we weren't going to resolve our differences, I walked out of the meeting.

I didn't care how the person leading the meeting felt about me, but I was embarrassed that Ian—a new member of the team with whom I would have to work in the future—had witnessed our clash. I telephoned Ian that afternoon and apologized. Fortunately, Ian was an easy-going Aussie and wasn't offended. Shortly thereafter, I invited Ian to join me for lunch so we could get better acquainted. We soon became good friends. I'm glad Ian gave me a second chance, because I know I didn't make a good first impression with him.

If someone irritates you at first, try to think of the most generous interpretation of his behavior. Perhaps he gets nervous when meeting new people. He also probably wants to make a good impression, particularly if he is somewhat intimidated or overly impressed by the other people in the room. He might try too hard to fit in or look good, and as a result he might come across as loud or self-aggrandizing. Give such a person another chance in a different environment. Perhaps he'll still be a jerk, but see if he repeats the behavior before you write him off.

Chapter 2

PROMISES, PROMISES

*Pearl #2: Honoring the commitments you
make to others will develop your reputation
as a reliable person and a good friend.*

How do you feel when someone promises to do something
for you or with you and then drops the ball? It's irritating,
whether this happens in your personal life or at work. It's especially
aggravating if you need that person to deliver before you can move on
with the next stage of a project. After someone lets you down a couple of
times, you are less likely to trust him. You're certainly not going to rely
on him to do something he promised, and you'll probably be surprised
if he really does deliver on a commitment.

One of my guiding principles is: Never make a commitment that
you know you cannot keep. I'm firmly in the camp of under-promising
and over-delivering. I practice this philosophy in my daily life, and I
practiced it when I was working at Kodak. I've especially tried to follow

this rule with my software consulting and training company, Process Impact. In a one-person company, there isn't anyone else to pick up the slack. If you make too many promises to too many clients, you're going to wear yourself out trying to deliver. And if you don't deliver, the client won't pay you. It's pretty simple.

I took a slight hit on my performance evaluation one year at Kodak because of my thoughtful attitude toward making commitments. My manager wrote, "Karl is somewhat selective in the assignments he accepts, but he always does an excellent job on those he undertakes." This was a backhanded compliment. His implication was that I didn't always accommodate my manager's requests. I was comfortable with that evaluation, though. We all need to manage our own workloads. You help no one if you keep taking on more responsibilities, only to fall farther and farther behind.

Occasionally you might make a commitment that you honestly think you can fulfill, but then things change and you're unable to deliver on your promise. If I discover that I cannot fulfill a commitment I've made, I tell the affected parties as early as possible. No one wants to hear bad news. The earlier they hear it, though, the more time they have to take the necessary corrective action. Here's an example of how that worked in practice.

In the 1970s and early 1980s, my favorite hobby was playing board war games. Having grown up on air force bases, I had developed a strong interest in military history, so wargaming was a natural fit for me. I began writing game reviews and articles on military history for magazines. In 1983, I got into personal computing, beginning with an Atari 800. I started writing articles for computing magazines—mostly tutorials—as I figured out how to do interesting things with the computer. My two hobbies intersected at one point.

I had agreed to review a new game for a wargaming magazine. But before I could play the game and begin figuring it out, the editor at one of the Atari magazines invited me to write a tutorial column. A column! Every magazine writer's dream is to have a column. I could write about whatever I wanted, with a guarantee that it would be published, and I'd get a steady income stream to boot. I was thrilled and eager to write more articles about Atari programming. But that game review I had promised to write was looming over my head. What to do?

I immediately mailed the game back to the wargaming magazine editor with an apologetic letter, explaining my situation. I felt bad about not being able to fulfill my commitment, and I was worried that the editor would be angry with me. Later, though, that editor told me, "You earned a lot of points around here when you returned that game and told us you couldn't write the review. Usually when I send out a game I don't get a review, and I don't get the game back." I hadn't felt that I was taking any extraordinary action, and I didn't expect such gratitude from the editor. If I said I was going to do something but then discovered I couldn't, what was there to do other than apologize and say I couldn't fulfill my obligation? I guess that's not the way all of their game reviewers operated, although it was the only course of action that seemed fair to me. That editor's comment taught me how important it is to be honest about the commitments you find you can't fulfill, even if you're embarrassed about it.

A recent encounter with a longtime friend showed how painful it can be when people don't honor their commitments. My wife and I had invited good friends I'll call Jerry and Suzanne to join us for a nice dinner out—our treat—for a triple celebration: Suzanne's birthday, Suzanne and Jerry's engagement, and our wedding anniversary. A few days prior to the dinner, Jerry called and said that Suzanne had to cancel. She wanted to participate on that same date in a special event with a different group of her female friends. In other words, Suzanne blew us off and didn't even have the courtesy to tell us herself. Poor Jerry was caught in the middle.

Suzanne had occasionally canceled plans with Chris in the past. Certainly, emergencies happen and sometimes plans must change. But that was not the case here. Suzanne said that that date was the only time all of her friends could connect for the event. Suzanne forgot that *she* was not available that day because she had already made the commitment to join us for dinner. Had she explained the situation to us and asked to reschedule, perhaps we could have worked it out. Instead, she asked Jerry to tell us.

Chris was especially upset. She felt that Suzanne's cancellation expressed something deeper: that their friendship was not very important. Chris explained her feelings so Suzanne knew what the problem was. Later, though, Suzanne wrote Chris a note professing that she was mystified as to what she had done wrong. Suzanne just didn't get it. Her actions severely damaged the long-term friendship among the four of us. She made her decision, but decisions have consequences.

Contemplate the commitments you make to your friends and colleagues. Are they realistic? How many of them do you deliver on? Are you generally reliable? If you find that you can't do something you promised, do you let the affected people know? Or do you hope they won't notice that you didn't follow through?

Here's another illustration. Last year, I injured my shoulder, wrist, and knee in a fall on a wet, slippery wheelchair ramp while I was on my Meals on Wheels delivery route. I asked a neighbor, a young man whom I had not met before, if he was interested in mowing my lawn for me. I knew he was mowing another neighbor's lawn and that he could use the money. "Sure," he said. We agreed that he would come over the next day. But he never showed up, he never called me, and I literally never saw the man again. That's just rude.

There are numerous reasons why people fail to fulfill commitments. Busy people forget, or they regard a "commitment" as being just a possibility, not a promise. Another reason is that people are often overly optimistic when estimating how long it will take to finish something. Everyone wants to be accommodating. Particularly in the business environment, we tend to give aggressive estimates because we don't want to look like slackers or incompetents. However, sometimes we don't really *estimate* how long it will take us to accomplish a task. Instead we make a *guess*, or we succumb to the pressure to deliver earlier than we think is realistically achievable. An externally imposed goal is not the same thing as a carefully thought-out estimate. Nobody wins when this happens on a regular basis.

In my view, the correct response to any request for an estimate is, "Let me get back to you on that." Instead of making a guess off the top of your head, think about it first. Identify the tasks you'd have to perform to complete that piece of work. Think about possible risks, bottlenecks, or dependencies on outside factors that might slow you down. Build a little slack into your estimate to account for the unavoidable uncertainties of life. This is just good project management. It applies to our personal lives as well as to our business activities.

Over time, I've worked hard to develop a reputation for delivering high-quality work when promised, usually before the agreed-upon deadline. If that means people don't always hear the commitments they want from me, I can live with that.

Chapter 3

DON'T SNEEZE ON YOUR SPOUSE

*Pearl #3: Showing consideration for the person who
is most important to you is more important than
running the risk of offending a friend or a stranger.*

Many years ago, before we were married, my wife and I had
close friends named Mike and Kathy who had been happily
married for years. It's easy for a couple who has been together for a
long time to take each other for granted, but we were impressed with
the respect and thoughtfulness Mike and Kathy still showed for each
other. One evening, Kathy described one of their simple philosophies
of marriage.

Suppose you and your partner are sitting around a dinner table
with several other people, perhaps a mix of friends and acquaintances.
Suddenly you feel an irrepressible need to sneeze. Which way do you
turn your head? Toward your partner, or toward the person on your
other side, whom you might not know? I suspect most people will

turn toward their partner, not wanting to offend a stranger, a casual acquaintance, or even a good friend. Kathy's point was: Why should you sneeze in the direction of the person who is most important to you in the world, if another alternative is available?

It's an interesting point. On the one hand, I don't wish to offend a third party by sneezing in their general direction, even if the sneeze is well contained in my napkin, fist, or elbow. However, whom should I be more concerned about offending? Don't I show more consideration and respect for my partner and our relationship if I turn my head away from her?

Naturally, I'd rather not offend anyone. If I can quickly get up from the table and not sneeze toward anybody, that's the best option. But I think it's less important to avoid offending a stranger or a friend than someone more dear to me. You can apply this courtesy to other aspects of your relationship, too. Simple considerations like opening the car door for your partner, offering her the last piece of chocolate or glass of wine, and knowing whether she prefers an aisle or interior seat at the theater, all send the message: "Your well-being and your happiness are important to me."

Ever since that conversation with Mike and Kathy, I've tried to keep my wife at the top of my priority list any time a potential trade-off arises between her and anyone else. If you have plans to do something with a friend, but your partner really wants to go out with you that night, maybe you should go out with your partner. The friend can wait.

It's a simple lesson, but for nearly a quarter of a century now, I've tried not to sneeze on my spouse.

Chapter 4

IT'S NOT ABOUT YOU

Pearl #4: Don't overreact to someone else's
decision if that decision is not really about you.

When I was in high school I had a friend named Mick, a great guy with many fine qualities. Mick was uncommonly mature for his age, self-motivated, and reliable. Late in high school, Mick got a new girlfriend named Diann. I didn't know Diann very well, but the two of them certainly got along well. Before long, they announced that they were getting married. Mick invited me to be an usher at his wedding.

I should have been honored. Instead, I was an idiot. I thought that Mick and Diann were getting married too soon and too young and that their marriage wouldn't stand much of a chance. Therefore, I decided to boycott their wedding. I declined Mick's invitation to be an usher.

This was in the early 1970s, when boycotts and protests were fashionable. I was a bit of a revolutionary activist back then myself, so this action was in character for me. It was also rash and foolish, and I

19

wish someone had talked me out of it. I failed to recognize that this wedding had nothing to do with me. I was simply a friend of the parties involved and had been invited to participate. It was their decision, it was their day, and I had no business disrupting it.

Well, the joke was on me. Mick accepted my decision with more grace than I had shown. I did boycott the wedding, although I stayed friends with Mick and Diann. And now, some thirty-eight years later, they are still happily married.

I've always regretted that decision. When I reconnected with Mick and Diann after many years, I was finally able to apologize for the foolish action of my youth. They graciously accepted my apology, which I appreciated. It was a long time ago, and at least I learned something from the experience. It's unfortunate that so often we must learn through our mistakes.

Sometimes people read more than is warranted into another person's personal decision or action. My friend Roger experienced this situation with his own family. Roger elected to have a vasectomy at the ripe young age of twenty-six. He had no children, had never wanted children, and was 100 percent certain that he never would want children. Thirty years later, he has never regretted that choice.

However, telling his family about the vasectomy didn't go over well. Roger's parents accepted his choice, although they thought he was being hasty and foolish and that eventually he would regret it. But his younger brother objected vehemently. For some reason, his brother took Roger's decision as a personal affront. The brother interpreted it as a slap in the family's face. He concluded that, by electing not to have children, Roger was saying that he didn't wish to carry on the family name.

Roger's brother was wrong. Choosing whether to have children is an intensely personal decision. It's the business of no one but the individual involved, and perhaps his or her life partner. Roger never considered how his family might react, because he didn't think his decision to have a vasectomy affected them in any way. Certainly, his family members were not entitled to a vote. Roger was not asking for their opinion or blessing. He was simply conveying a significant life decision that he had made to the rest of his family. Roger's brother didn't recognize that this decision wasn't about him or the rest of Roger's family. It was just about Roger.

In everyday conversations, we can also forget that it isn't always about us. For example, when you're talking with someone who describes an experience he recently had, it's almost automatic to respond with your own story on that same topic. Your buddy tells you about the great score he shot on the golf course today. Instead of congratulating him, your first reaction is to tell him about *your* best day on the links. But it's his story, not yours. You can tell him about your own greatest round another time. Let him revel in the enthusiasm of his moment; share it with him. The same can happen when you're relating a sad tale about an illness to a friend. "Is that right?" your friend says. "Well, my second cousin had *both* arms, plus one leg, fall off from leprosy!" You really don't want to hear about someone else's worst-case scenario when you're concerned about your own health or that of a loved one.

I'm guilty of this kind of response during conversations. Despite being aware of the phenomenon, I sometimes blurt out my own story before I can stop myself. As soon as I realize that I've done it again, I mentally kick myself and then really try to focus on what my friend is saying. When I'm sharing an experience of my own, I try to remember to give the other person opportunities to participate, by asking questions like, "Have you ever done something like that?" A conversation should be a dialogue, not a soliloquy.

Perhaps you know someone who is a particularly good listener. Good listeners let you tell your tales uninterrupted. They share your excitement. They don't interject with "Oh, yeah? Let me tell you about..."

and then go on to expound about their personal experiences. They don't try to compete with you or top your achievement. They simply listen, smile, nod, and make appropriate responses at the right times. Good listeners make you feel like they really care about your experiences and your happiness.

My friend Norm is one of these great listeners. He'll lean in toward me attentively, blue eyes sparkling, and ask questions that encourage me to share the full energy of my story. I always feel as if Norm is intensely interested in whatever I have to say, even if it is something mundane. He's a master of "active listening."

We all appreciate this sort of positive interaction with people. It's great to feel that others genuinely care about us and share our enthusiasm. I try to show this same kind of respect to my conversation partners and remind myself that the discussion is not about me but about them. I don't always achieve that goal. I will keep trying.

Chapter 5

LIFE'S TOO SHORT

*Pearl #5: Life is too short to let old rifts and
perceived offenses keep family members or friends apart.*

any years ago I had a falling out with a close relative I'll call
Mary, who had taken offense to a family-oriented decision
I had made. I could see her point. I probably didn't communicate my
decision to my family very well, but I thought she had overreacted.
Mary wrote me a hateful letter that shocked and angered me. I did not
respond. A few weeks later, Mary called and began chatting with me as
if nothing had happened. I told her, "Unless you're calling to apologize
for your letter, we have nothing to talk about." She paused a moment
and then hung up on me. We didn't speak for a long time. I said nothing
about our rift to other members of our family, and I never knew if Mary
shared our disagreement with anyone.

Some months later, my father came to the city where I lived for a
short visit. At one point during his stay, he said, "I don't know what the

problem is between you and Mary, but I wish you two would work it out. Life's too short."

I'm not sure how or what he knew about our conflict, but my father was right. Life is too short to propagate a feud indefinitely. Mary and I gradually began communicating again and eventually got back on good terms. We never mentioned the issue again. Now, decades later, we get along just fine. We're both glad we got over our rift long ago.

I'm normally not one to carry a grudge for long. If I become angry with someone, I usually get over it pretty quickly. If I'm the transgressor, I'm apt to apologize shortly after I've calmed down and realized what I've done or said. Not everyone is like that, though. Sometimes breakups between friends or feuds among family members can last for years, for decades, or until death do us part.

It's hard to swallow your pride and reach out to someone you have wronged or who has wronged you. You never know how that person will react. Perhaps she will be delighted to meet you halfway, but maybe she'll still be as angry as ever. Maybe making contact will just reopen a festering wound. You don't know what to expect.

A friend of mine, Marcus, experienced an even more severe familial rift. Marcus's mother became very ill a few years ago. He flew across the country and spent several weeks helping one of his sisters, who had been living with their mother, take care of her. Perhaps it was the intrusion of Marcus into the mother-daughter dynamic, or it could have been the stress of having a third person living in the house during a crisis, but clashes arose between Marcus and his sister. Marcus felt that his sister did not appreciate the effort he was making to help around the house, to drive his mother to doctors' appointments, to shop for groceries, and so forth. His sister exhibited various passive-aggressive behaviors (along with out-and-out aggressive behaviors) that upset Marcus. Eventually he went back home, exhausted both mentally and physically from his mother's illness and the stress of interacting with his unappreciative sister.

Marcus's mother died a few months later. Her passing hit the family hard. Marcus and his siblings spent a lot of time grieving. One day, though, a comment from one of Marcus's brothers about the care-giving sister struck a nerve. Marcus wrote his brother a long letter in which he detailed the time he had spent helping his mother and the lousy way their sister had treated him. Despite the fact that Marcus asked his brother to keep the letter to himself, his brother showed the letter to both the offending sister and another sibling. The conflict escalated. Vicious letters flew back and forth, relationships were severed, and finally mail was being returned unopened. The six middle-aged children wound up polarized, three in each opposing camp. This was a chasm, not just a rift.

As time passes, you expect that grief will take its natural course, people will calm down, anger will abate, and long-standing relationships will reestablish themselves. That hasn't happened in this family yet. Marcus has taken some tentative steps, such as sending a congratulatory card to one sister in the other camp on a milestone wedding anniversary. He received a cordial, but certainly not warm, reply, and they haven't communicated since. It's not clear how the situation will resolve, if at all. It would be a shame if these siblings were not able to have civil relationships again, because they've always been a close-knit family.

I think Marcus would like to reestablish contact with his siblings and his nieces and nephews. But it's hard to know how to cross that gulf. You don't know whether a friendly hand awaits you on the other side or if you'll be shoved back into the abyss. Do you take the risk of being hurt again, or do you hang onto that grudge, perhaps far longer than anyone wants?

If you've burned any bridges with family members or close friends, maybe it's time to get over it. It's true that time heals most (though not all) wounds, but you have to let time do its job. Eventually, it doesn't matter who did what or said what to whom and why. In most cases, the right thing to do is to give up the grudge and try to get back on good terms with the people who have always been close to you. If you can, you put the incident behind you—maybe you don't even mention it again—and you move on. It's never too late to build a new bridge and heal a broken relationship. Life is too short to stay bitter and angry forever.

Chapter 6

GIRLS AND STREETCARS

Pearl #6: If your parents do not teach you how to succeed in relationships with others, you will have to learn those skills on your own, often through painful experience.

*M*y father had numerous fine qualities. He was a self-made man, rising out of an abusive childhood in poverty to spend more than twenty years in the Air Force and then achieve a successful career in the private sector as a data processing manager for two large companies. He developed an impressive variety of interests and skills: traveling, camping, leatherwork, clarinet, cars and engines, auto racing, construction around the house, gardening, and more.

Despite his exceptional store of knowledge and experiences, my father was unable to help me develop skills for perhaps the most important aspect of being a mature and happy adult: relationships with other people. Instead, I had to learn how to navigate interpersonal relationships largely on my own. It took a long time, many mistakes, and much depression.

Like most teenaged boys, I struggled to find girlfriends. I completely skipped the stage most boys go through where they hate girls—I always loved girls. Usually, however, the ones I was attracted to didn't like me back. (My mother said she had the same problem with boys when she was young, so I'm guessing my situation was not unique.) Occasionally, I did manage to land a girlfriend. Of course, all such relationships come to an end, and I was traumatized any time a girl broke up with me. Typical teenage angst.

When I was feeling low, I could always talk to my mother. She was sympathetic. But Dad was not much help. The sole piece of guidance I received from him about relationships with women was: "Girls are just like streetcars. If you missed this one, another one will come along soon."* I can't tell you how many times I heard that after a breakup. It was never the least bit consoling or helpful, even if it contained an element of truth.

Developing and sustaining personal and business relationships with members of both sexes was challenging for me for years. I'm sure my lack of ability in this area contributed to two failed marriages by the time I was thirty-two and the departure of a roommate who was delighted to move out of an apartment we shared for nine months. (Sorry, Rich; I'm better now.) I matured late; more parental guidance as an adolescent would have been helpful.

In later years, I realized that I had received virtually no coaching from my father about interpersonal relationships or about how to interact with people of both genders in a constructive and mature

---

* It's possible that my father was fond of this saying because of the storybook way he met my mother. He was living in Denver, Colorado. My mother had moved there after high school to look for a job. One day as she stepped off a streetcar, the heel of her shoe got caught in the grate on the streetcar steps. The heel snapped off, and she fell. Dad caught her, and they took it from there. Unfortunately, there weren't any streetcars in Boise, Idaho, when I was a teenager, so this didn't seem like a good way to meet girls.

fashion. Dad was always free with "advice" when I was a teenager, but this typically involved telling me to get a haircut with disturbing frequency. I did get a little bit of good advice from my father about corporate management. For example, he once told me that the first thing he did whenever he moved into a new management role was to start looking for his replacement and grooming that individual to take his place. That is, succession planning was a top priority for him. This is not bad information, but it's pretty much all I remember getting along these lines.

Dad knew a lot about cars. He taught me how to rebuild a damaged carburetor but not a damaged relationship. Despite the fact that he had become skilled in leadership through his military and corporate careers, he couldn't show me how he won the hearts and minds of his colleagues and subordinates, how he was able to align people with his vision of a better future, or how to resolve conflicts. These are all skills I would need to become an effective and compassionate leader and partner in later life. He taught me nothing about how to steer your own managers to your advantage, a useful survival skill in any organization. I eventually figured out some of these things on my own and by picking up tips from colleagues and managers in my professional career. Learning them earlier would have saved me—and people around me—considerable unhappiness and frustration.

Schools teach courses on many topics, but I don't remember taking any classes that dealt with emotions, consideration of others, or relationships and their associated joys and traumas. If you don't learn these things from your parents, teachers, or other mentors, then you're going to have to stumble through these growing pains on your own. Perhaps you'll find some guidance from an older adolescent (although often this is in the vein of assorted sexual folklore) or a trusted relative.

Eventually I did get better at all that stuff, but I certainly wish I had received more coaching and guidance regarding interpersonal relationships from my father, especially at an early age. Being a typical teenager, I might not have been receptive to his input. But it could have helped. Although it's unfortunate that my father didn't teach me more about how to cultivate and nurture relationships, I'm grateful that I was able to learn—if not master—these skills on my own nonetheless.

Part 2

PERSONAL PEARLS

It's rewarding to learn a principle or technique that can help you communicate more easily with others or do a better job at work. It's a different matter to learn something about yourself: something that makes you think about who you are, how you came to be that way, and what changes you'd like to make. That's the focus of the pearls of wisdom in this section.

Several of these stories deal with how we view ourselves compared with how others view us. It can be shocking to learn how our values and personality come across to other people. Other pearls came to me as personal realizations during certain small encounters. Each was just a moment in time when a powerful insight flashed into my mind in the midst of an otherwise ordinary experience.

Some of these stories were painful to write. They took me back to earlier days and to some not-so-fond memories. I'm not proud of how I behaved in some of these situations. But each experience taught me a valuable lesson. I share these lessons hoping that you will benefit from them and that they'll motivate you to search your memory for similar experiences and insights. Divining such lessons could make your life happier and more satisfying.

I wish there had been an easier way to learn about myself than by getting so many things wrong the first time and making course corrections. I never received a "Handbook of Karl" to help me figure out who I was and how to operate me. Instead it took trial and error—more error than I would have liked. I hope your journey to self-realization is smoother.

Chapter 7

INTROVERTED IS
SOMETHING YOU ARE

*Pearl #7: Understanding and accepting the nature of your
personality will help you interact comfortably with others
and understand the behaviors of those who are close to you.*

I gave my first presentation at a software development conference
in 1991. It was well received, so I gradually began giving more
talks at conferences and meetings of professional software organizations.
Public speaking is one of the greatest fears for most people. The fear
even has a name: glossophobia. At first I experienced a normal level of
anxiety before each presentation, but I soon became comfortable behind
the microphone. I felt confident because I knew my material and I knew
the audience wanted to hear it.

One benefit of speaking at conferences is that you get to meet a lot of
interesting, smart, and sometimes famous people. One of those people
was Larry, a man ten years older than me who was highly respected in

the software industry as a thinker, author, and consultant. Interestingly, he had also spent some time as a family therapist. Larry planned and led some of the conferences at which I regularly spoke. One afternoon Larry and I were chatting over a glass of wine following a conference. He remarked that my speaking career was coming along nicely. "Thanks," I said. "I used to be introverted, but now I'm pretty comfortable giving these presentations."

Larry corrected me gently. "No, Karl, introverted is not something you *were*. Introverted is something you *are*."

Larry had my attention. I had always viewed myself as an introvert. I'm not shy, but I've never been surrounded by friends or on the A-list for parties. True, I've always enjoyed standing in front of a group and sharing information on a topic I'm passionate about. I had mistakenly thought that my increasing level of comfort on stage meant that my personality was moving from introverted toward extroverted. Larry's message was basically: once an introvert, always an introvert. It's an integral part of your makeup.

I didn't have a clear understanding of the difference between an extrovert and an introvert at that point, so I did some research. I learned that extroverts tend to be outgoing, gregarious, and assertive, whereas introverts typically are more reserved. Introverts are not necessarily shy or loners, but they are satisfied with having fewer friends and they prefer less social activities. The key message here is that the spectrum of introversion and extroversion is a matter of *social preference* regarding the comfort level an individual has when interacting with others. Extroverts typically obtain gratification through activities external to themselves, such as interacting with people in social gatherings. Introverts, on the other hand, are more internally focused, often reserved in group settings and more likely to obtain pleasure from solitary activities.

You can spot the difference between public speakers who tend toward introversion and those who tend toward extroversion by the way they interact with the audience before the presentation begins. There's an awkward few moments between the time you've set up your laptop and microphone and are ready to go and the scheduled start time for the presentation. I generally hang by myself off to the side during that short period, perhaps chatting with the people nearest me. But some of my colleagues really work the crowd. They walk up and down the aisles, introducing themselves and shaking hands. They ask the attendees where they work, what they do, why they chose to come to this presentation, and what they hope to get out of it. Diving into the crowd like that just doesn't feel comfortable to me. This seems like a classic distinction of behavior between introverts and extroverts.

Another way my tendency toward introversion shows up at conferences is during mealtimes. When I walk into the hall where lunch is served, I might opt to sit at a table where I spot a familiar face. More often, though, I will sit at a table by myself. Other people will likely join me as the room fills up, and that's fine by me. I'm happy to interact with whomever is around me, but I do not usually seek out that interaction. I also try to grab some downtime by myself at lunch when I'm teaching a full-day class. I'm not being antisocial, just regrouping and resting my voice. And after a long day delivering a training class, I need an hour or so alone in my hotel room to wind down and recharge before I'm ready to meet people from the class for dinner. This is typical introvert behavior.

One way to locate an individual's position on the introversion-extroversion spectrum is through a Myers-Briggs Type Indicator personality inventory. When I took this assessment several years ago, I came out just about halfway along the continuum. That is, I demonstrate characteristics of both introverts and extroverts, a personality trait called ambiversion. I can see that in myself. I enjoy social activities like wine tasting, and I like to collaborate with other people in various capacities, but I'm also perfectly happy doing things by myself. Similarly, I need to have some time alone once in a while. My father was the same way. Often personality tendencies are hereditary.

Consider my musical activities. I really enjoy playing guitar in a band, which I rarely get an opportunity to do these days. But I've also had great fun in recent years recording songs entirely by myself, figuring out all the parts and recording every instrumental and vocal track on my own. (The name of my band is *Me 3!* because the musicians are Me, Myself, and I.) It would be fun to blend other musical styles and voices with my own on these songs, if the opportunity arises. There are some advantages to playing in a "band" all by yourself, though. Everybody is available to practice at the same time, they all like the same songs, and they all have the same quality standards.

Sometimes people surprise you. I had always considered my wife to be an extrovert. Chris is outgoing and comfortable with people. She's funny and bubbly, cheerful and friendly. These characteristics leapt out at me every time I walked into her office when we were both working at Kodak. However, she really is an introvert! There is nothing Chris would rather do than read, the ultimate solitary activity. She feels like an introvert, but she was able to pose as an extrovert when it was necessary for her job. Once I knew this about Chris, I had a better understanding of the situations in which she felt most comfortable and the ways she liked to spend her time. I knew why she enjoyed reading so much and why she wasn't big on loud parties and other social activities.

"Know thyself" is a proverb inscribed in the Greek temple of Apollo at Delphi, dating from about the sixth century BC. It is indeed helpful to understand the fundamental characteristics of our own personalities and the personalities of people close to us. It's a good idea to occasionally stretch out of our comfort zone to gain new experiences, and perhaps even enjoyment, that we wouldn't otherwise have. However, our basic natures dictate the ways we prefer to spend our time.

Do you act differently in different social settings? What kinds of settings feel most comfortable to you? Do you prefer raucous parties with many intriguing strangers to meet, or would you rather just have a quiet cup of coffee with a friend or two? It probably helps to be a strong extrovert if you're a car salesman. In contrast, scientists and software geeks (I'm guilty on both counts) often are stereotyped as extreme introverts, being perfectly comfortable in the lab or at the keyboard but not terribly engaged with the rest of the human race. There's a bit of truth to this, but in reality, few people are pegged clear over to one extreme or the other on the introversion-extroversion scale.

Understanding and respecting the social preferences of people around you also is valuable. When I was a manager, I once supervised a woman in her early thirties who was both extremely introverted and very shy. She rarely spoke up in a group setting. However, I had come to respect her ideas, and I really wanted to hear her contributions to our team's discussions. I tried to think of ways to make it comfortable and safe for her to share her thoughts in group meetings. If she just couldn't do that, I would pick her brain afterward because her opinions were important to me.

That comment Larry made to me after the software conference helped me realize that the introverted side of my personality is still around, even though I also enjoy public speaking. I'm comfortable giving presentations to audiences ranging in size from one to thousands. I think I'm a dynamic and entertaining speaker. But when I get off the stage, I instinctively dial it back. One of my colleagues once remarked, "You're like two different people: one when you're presenting and another when you're not." In reality, I'm always me, both onstage and off, but there is more than one "me" in here.

Chapter 8

ON THE TREADMILL FOR LIFE

Pearl #8: Even if you hate team sports or were hopelessly unathletic as a child, you can learn to enjoy regular exercise and reap its many benefits.

year after I moved to Rochester, New York, in 1979, I went to see an allergy specialist. I've suffered from respiratory allergies all my life, as do most members of my family. The allergist examined me and arranged for skin testing. I wound up being allergic to seventy-four of the seventy-seven allergens for which I was tested. I had the most impressive skin response to ragweed that the allergist's office had ever seen. It itched for two weeks; I was very proud. However, as we discussed my exam results, Dr. Susan said that my lungs weren't working quite as well as she thought they should. "Do you get any exercise at all?" she asked.

I was embarrassed to admit that no, I didn't. Besides throwing a football or baseball around sometimes with my father and brother, and the occasional neighborhood pickup game, athletics had never been a part of my life. I had taken the requisite physical education classes in seventh and tenth grades and hated every minute of them. I hadn't played any youth sports, except for a handful of Little League baseball games when I was ten or eleven. I was younger than my classmates because I had skipped a grade; this didn't help with my prowess or confidence on the field.

My athletic ineptitude, combined with my age, became particularly problematic in tenth grade. On the first day of class, my gym teacher, a kindly fellow, told the students to use one physical performance tracking chart if we had already turned sixteen years old and to use a different chart if we were younger than that. When I told him that I was thirteen, he looked at me in amazement. "You'll have to use the fifteen-year-old chart," he said. Luckily he took it easy on me throughout the year, knowing that I was doing my best.

I tried hard in all the gym activities, but it was a tough go. Although I was tall for my age, I was skinny, completely lacking in athletic ability and experience, and hopelessly uncoordinated. I never tripped over the lines painted on the gym floor, although I did stumble once. It was difficult to compete with kids with hair on their chests who had been playing sports for years. It was discouraging always to be the last kid picked for every sports team, even after the fat kid. At least the fat kid was popular. Team captains tried to avoid getting stuck with Wiegers. This experience did not instill in me a lasting desire to participate voluntarily in team sports. Other than a tennis match once in a while or the rare football game with friends (which always left me incredibly sore because I knew nothing about warming up, stretching, or cooling down), I did no real exercising in college or graduate school.

But there's good news! Admitting to the allergist that I didn't get any exercise was one of those "Aha!" moments that changed the direction of my life. At that time I shared my office at Kodak with Tony, another scientist who had started working at the company around the same time I had. Tony was incredibly energetic. He worked out at the Kodak gym regularly, served on a volunteer ambulance crew after work, explored caves on weekends, and on and on. I began going to the Kodak gym three days a week with Tony. We jogged together, and he helped me establish a weightlifting routine. Tony gave me much helpful advice about proper exercising techniques. I gradually increased the distance I could run and the weight I could lift. It was rewarding to see my strength, stamina, and self-confidence improve. Maybe I wouldn't have to be a 137-pound weakling forever.

After that, physical fitness became an important part of my life, and I have exercised regularly for more than thirty years. Chris and I have a workout room in our house that contains a treadmill, stationary bike, rowing machine, stair-stepper, two weight machines, and a large collection of dumbbells. We also have the most important pieces of exercise equipment: cable TV and a DVD player. Unfortunately, my muscles have always been able to handle more weight and repetitions than my joints could tolerate. But I still try to push myself—while striving to avoid injuries—and I work out an average of five days a week. If I go more than two days without some kind of physical activity, I miss it. Even without experiencing the legendary endorphin rush that comes from intense exercise, I enjoy each workout and I feel better for it. Exercise has done great things for my cardiovascular and pulmonary health; it's also helped keep my weight down to just a few pounds above what I weighed in high school.

Being in better physical shape is great, but I'll still never be an athlete and I don't play organized sports. I did play softball on a low-level company league at Kodak in my early thirties, partly because the main goal of the team was to drink beer after each game. I had no ability or instinct for the game, although my batting wasn't horrible. I played catcher because I was too inept to play any other position. I could catch okay, but when I threw the ball back to the pitcher, the entire infield had to be prepared. You never knew where the ball was going to end up—no exaggeration. My teammates were quite tolerant of my athletic limitations, although I noticed that no one was disappointed when I dropped out after five years.

Every little bit of exercise helps. As we get older, most of us are less likely to exercise, and it takes a bigger toll on our muscles and joints when we do. But I have a theory about fitness as we age. Some of you are probably familiar with this experience: You walk upstairs, say, to brush your teeth. Then you get distracted by some entirely unrelated activity, do that instead, and start to walk back down the stairs. About halfway down you recall that you had gone upstairs in the first place to do... something. What was it? Oh, yes—you were going to brush your teeth. So you turn around, climb back up the stairs, brush your teeth, and walk back downstairs to continue your evening. My theory is that this modest forgetfulness is nature's way of keeping you active as you age, by requiring you to walk around more than you did when your memory was more reliable.

Thanks to the admonition implied by my allergist's simple question, I was motivated to exchange my sedentary lifestyle for one that involves vigorous activity for at least a few hours a week. Having friends I could exercise with at first really helped sustain my momentum until I became entirely self-motivated. So I offer a big "Thank you" to Dr. Susan and my friends Tony, John, and Mike for instilling in me a lasting appreciation for physical fitness and helping me overcome the distaste left by high school PE class.

Do you prefer to hang around the gym or the couch? If you're a couch person, it's never too late to start moving more. I see a lot of people out for early-morning walks on the big hill that I live on: with dogs, with friends, or on their own. Half a mile from my house is another hill, a nature preserve with numerous hiking trails. It's a lovely place to work up a sweat. On a morning stroll you might even see the occasional deer.

Do you have a safe place to walk and a friend to walk with? Exercising with a friend turns a chore into a social encounter. Start slowly and be sure to incorporate warm-up, stretching, and cool-down activities into your workout. Nothing destroys exercise motivation faster than pain.

Try to set a routine. If you just promise yourself, "I'll exercise three times this week," you probably won't. There are too many other time- and energy-sucking distractions. But if you schedule some exercise sessions for specific days and times, you'll be much more likely to do them. My sixty-three-year-old brother-in-law never exercised until about fifteen years ago. Now he puts in an hour or more before work nearly every day. That impresses the heck out of me. I can really see the benefits, too.

Many people join a fitness center or health club, hoping that it will motivate them to exercise more. Sometimes it does, but often it's just money down the drain. Here's an easy three-step way to get many of the benefits of a health club—for free:

Step 1: Find a health club near you, preferably a mile or two away.

Step 2: Schedule three one-hour sessions on your weekly calendar, any time of day that's convenient for you.

Step 3: At each scheduled time, walk to the health club, turn around, and walk back. Eventually you can run there, turn around, and run home.

You don't have to enter the health club to get the full benefits from this free exercise program. You don't even have to pay to join the club. Such a deal!

Chapter 9

LOOK! UP IN THE SKY! IT'S PERFECTMAN!

Pearl #9: Perfectionists will make their lives—and the lives of those around them—easier if they know when situations actually demand perfection and when "good enough" will do.

Some people would describe me as a perfectionist. That's not far off, but it's not quite right. I used to be more of a perfectionist; I'm a little better now, although I still have a ways to go. A Perfectman is more of a super-nuisance than a superhero. So instead of expecting everything to be perfect, I try to follow this philosophy: "Strive for perfection; settle for excellence."

I do have high standards, and I don't apologize for that. I expect a lot from myself, at least in certain arenas. For example, when I'm teaching a class in my everyday disguise as a mild-mannered software consultant, I always do the best job I possibly can. It doesn't matter if I've taught that same class more than a hundred times and it's incredibly boring to me now. That's my problem, not the audience's problem. The students in the class are entitled to the best presentation I can deliver that day, so that's what I strive to give them.

I don't have such high expectations of myself in other areas. I'm good at a few activities, but I'm less skilled or even completely inept when it comes to others. Construction projects around the house, for instance, are not my strong suit. Expecting perfection of myself in this area would be ludicrous. For such projects, I drop my standards down to "good enough." If that really *isn't* good enough to solve the problem, I'll bring in a professional to take care of it.

Perfection is more important in some situations than in others. I like to write and record songs, but I know my limitations. I'm not a brilliant songwriter, I'm not a fantastic guitarist, and I'm not a good singer. Through the miracles of modern recording and production software, I can compensate for some of my shortcomings and create songs that sound pretty good, if I do say so myself. I get a kick out of the composing, recording, and production process. It's a hobby, not a living. I'm just having a good time making music. I try to do the best job I can with the songs, but I'm not devastated if my efforts don't meet professional standards. Besides, you can never make a song—or a book—perfect. (Ironically, my most recent song is titled "Perfect," but it doesn't have anything to do with the theme of this chapter.) There's always something else you could tweak. At some point, you just have to declare victory and move on with your life.

I also expect a lot from others. I don't have much patience for either incompetence or incompetents, which does not seem unreasonable to me. If I send my local newspaper money for a subscription, I expect them to deliver my paper every day. If I hire professional roofers to repair the hole in my roof, it shouldn't leak anymore. Why should I expect less?

Last year I hired a handyman to replace a rotted exterior door that accesses the crawl space under my house. He sized up the job and concluded that he could handle it. Dan showed up on time, he seemed to know what he was doing, and the door looked sharp when he was done. However, when I tried to open the door a few months later, it was stuck fast. When the handyman installed it, he didn't allow enough clearance around the frame. The door expanded as it absorbed moisture in the wet Portland winter and was completely jammed into the frame. It took me a couple of hours to work the door open, followed by more hours to sand it down to fit properly and to repaint it.

But Dan disavowed any responsibility for the problem. He claimed that I had told him I wanted a snug fit around the door, which wasn't true. And even if I had said I wanted a snug fit, it's his professional responsibility to make the door serve its intended purpose. I didn't expect the door to be perfect, but I certainly expected it to open and close. That's kind of the point of a door. The handyman's work fell short of adequacy, let alone excellence, let alone perfection.

Being a perfectionist is hard. You set yourself up for disappointment at every turn, because people are not perfect, mechanical things are not perfect, and institutions are not perfect. I realize this. Still, I often believe things can be better than they are, better than we accept, and better than we demand. If you set perfection as a firm goal in life, either for yourself or for others, you will be frustrated more often than not. But if you set perfection as more of a hypothetical target and just aim for high quality, falling short may still leave you in the realm of excellence. That's nearly always a fine outcome.

Perfectionists are hard on the people around them too. They establish a reputation for incessant complaining, for being hypercritical and impossible to please. Consequently, any suggestion, observation, comment, or request Perfectman makes can come across as a scathing criticism, even when it's not intended that way. Thick-skinned people might not take the perfectionist's unreasonable expectations seriously. More sensitive people, though, will be hurt and will resent Perfectman's "suggestions." I regret the times I've inflicted this kind of pain on the people around me, and I keep trying to do better.

If you are a perfectionist, it can be liberating when the world pops your bubble. You buy a new car and it's gorgeous, not a mark on it. Of course, you don't want a door ding. So at first you park at the far end of the parking lot, well away from other vehicles. Or maybe you take the "I'm more important than you are" jerk approach and park diagonally across two spaces to make sure no one else's car door could possibly touch your baby. However, despite your best efforts, your flawless car eventually is going to pick up a little scratch or a tiny dent. When this happens, you're free! You can start acting like a normal automobile owner again.

Like many high-achieving students, I hoped to get straight As in college. I put a lot of pressure on myself, and I studied hard. Then I got my first B; I remember it well. This brought a sense of freedom, because then I didn't have to worry about trying to be perfect anymore. I still did the best job I possibly could in my schoolwork, but this relieved some of my internally generated pressure.

Parents sometimes don't realize how much stress they impose on their children by setting impossibly high goals. Many a child has felt like a failure because she didn't measure up to a parent's perfectionist ideal. The philosophy "Strive for perfection; settle for excellence" can perhaps reduce that stress, while maintaining the expectation of aiming high and doing good work.

If you're like me and expect much from yourself and others, you might consider whether these expectations are unreasonable or unrealistic. Think about easing off a little. Consider which situations really do demand perfection (performing surgery comes to mind), which ones will be just fine with mere excellence, and the situations for which "good enough" will suffice. It took me a long time to learn this lesson; I will probably never master it. It's in my bones to want everything to be just so. If perfectionists can channel their unrealistic demands into an expectation of high quality and even excellence, we'll all be happier.

Chapter 10

IT'S YOUR BODY, IT'S YOUR LIFE

Pearl #10: To be a good medical "customer," it's important to forge collaborative partnerships with your doctors; you must take some responsibility for your own health care.

When I was twenty-five, I went to see a doctor for a routine physical exam. My new internist, Dr. Art, was just a few years older than me. As we discussed my medical history and issues, I mentioned that I suffered from chronic respiratory allergies. I named some of the medications I had taken in the past, including an antihistamine called Actifed. Dr. Art asked, "Would you like a prescription for Actifed?"

I was surprised that Dr. Art asked me if I wanted a particular medication rather than merely handing me a prescription for whatever he thought was the right drug for me. This doctor was treating me like an intelligent adult and engaging me in making decisions about my health care. That was the first time any doctor I'd seen had ever done that. I was accustomed to simply accepting whatever treatment or tests the physician offered. I liked this approach better.

This encounter forged my belief that medical care must involve a collaborative partnership between you and your care providers. It's not all your responsibility, but it's not entirely up to the doctor to keep you hale and hearty either. You have to do your fair share. I appreciated Dr. Art's collaborative approach and accepted his offer of the Actifed prescription. Dr. Art remained my primary care physician until he moved to another city eighteen years later. He was the best doctor I've ever had.

Some patients treat their doctor's word as gospel. They expect the doctor to have all the answers—and to ask the patient all the right questions. They hope the doctor remembers all the details of their previous visits. They take whatever medications he prescribes without question. Then, after the doctor breezes out of the examination room, these patients think of the other questions they meant to ask. Better make another appointment.

That's one extreme. Other patients scour the Internet and medical books for everything they can learn about the symptoms they're experiencing and attempt to diagnose their condition themselves. They look into tests, investigate treatments, and read advertisements for new drugs before they go to the doctor. They tell the doctor about the problem, their diagnosis, and what tests and treatments they want. In the meantime, they've probably terrified themselves by learning about all the ghastly (but low-probability) diseases they could have. At that point, they just want the doctor to rubber-stamp the treatment plan they already came up with.

As with many things in life, finding a sensible balance point between these two extremes is best. I like to take a lot of responsibility for my own health care, but I leave the expertise to the experts. I do read about medical news in mainstream magazines, newspapers, and Web sites. However, I expect my doctor to read more and to monitor authoritative studies of whether, say, taking large doses of a particular vitamin is a good idea. I expect the physician to know whether a routine PSA blood test to screen for prostate cancer is a useful and cost-effective (for me, not for his practice) test to perform when I have my annual physical exam.

I want my doctors to engage me in the assessment of my health and the most appropriate treatments I may need. I appreciate finding a doctor who treats me like a responsible and knowledgeable adult and who gives me choices instead of just telling me what he's going to do or what I should do for myself. Dr. Art interacted with me in that fashion. I'm happy that my current primary care physician, Dr. Gary, is the same way. If he weren't, I'd find another doctor.

Most of the time, I enjoy good health. However, occasionally I have a medical issue that needs to be checked out. Several doctors have told me that I seemed unusually well-informed when I described my symptoms precisely and in medical terms. Most patients are probably more passive when it comes to their medical care. I want to know about the options and the possibilities. I don't want my doctor keeping secrets from me. It's my body, and it's my life. I'm entitled to whatever information and ideas my medical providers might have about my health.

Perhaps it's easier for me because I am organized and analytical by nature. I also am educated as a scientist and medical jargon doesn't intimidate me. When I see my doctor for a routine physical every year, I prepare a one-page write-up so we can spend our limited time together as efficiently and effectively as possible. My write-up lists medications I take, including vitamins, with their dosages and frequency. We can discuss whether these medications and supplements are appropriate based on my age, my health, and current medical research. I list the prescriptions that I need refilled. My one-pager itemizes anything relevant to my health from the previous year, including exercise levels, acute illnesses such as colds, and any other conditions he should check out. I give the doctor the dates and results of any other medical care I've received in the previous year, including routine eye care and dental exams. Finally, I list any questions I wish to discuss. I want my doctor to have a holistic picture of my health so he can give me the best care possible. Dr. Gary seems to appreciate getting this information in a condensed and organized fashion instead of piecemeal through dialogue. As a result, we get to spend more time discussing my specific concerns.

Most of my interactions with medical professionals have been fine. However, sometimes things don't go so well. When I was thirty-two, I underwent knee surgery to remove torn cartilage. (How it got torn remains a mystery.) The surgeon appeared competent, but his patient management practices were sorely deficient. The hospital's procedures weren't much better.

This was my first experience with general anesthesia. When I woke up after the surgery—which I really did not want to do; I was perfectly happy being asleep—the room was moving, my knee was heavily bandaged, and I felt queasy and groggy. The nurse came in and said, "Now let's go learn how to use crutches." I had never been on crutches before. Do you think maybe they could have asked me to visit the physical therapy facility a few days *before* the surgery to get fitted for crutches and learn to use them? Walking on crutches is tricky enough without having both the room and your stomach spinning.

Apparently, just before the operation, the surgeon had told me to make an appointment to come in for a follow-up exam. I do not remember this. Amnesia is a well-known consequence of general anesthesia. You would think the surgeon would know that and provide written—not verbal—instructions for follow-up care. When I did get back to see him a few days later, he said everything was coming along fine. Then he gave me the only instructions I ever got for the physical therapy and rehabilitation of my poor knee: "I'd like you to start lifting some weights with your leg now." Okay, I had a few questions. What kind of motions? How much weight? How many repetitions? How many times a day? For how many days? How fast should I build up to more weight? And on and on. The surgeon never recommended I see a physical therapist, never gave me any rehab guidance at all beyond "start lifting some weights." At that time, I wasn't savvy enough to raise these sorts of questions with him, but I wouldn't make that mistake again now.

I'm willing to take quite a bit of responsibility for my own health care, but come on, people, work with me here! I had to write a couple of customer complaint letters to the hospital and to the surgeon to describe my displeasure. I didn't just gripe: I also suggested specific changes they could make that might work better, at least based on my one data point of experience. To their credit, the hospital staff took me seriously. A head nurse sent me a reply that acknowledged my concerns and outlined some changes they planned to make, such as practicing with crutches prior to surgery. However, the surgeon never responded to my letter.

If you have an unsatisfactory experience with a medical professional, say so. They're all trying to do the best job they can, but, like all of us, they often aren't fully aware of how they come across to others. Medical caregivers might call us "patients," but really we are their customers and they are our service providers. Patients are entitled to expect the same high level of quality that all customers should expect from their suppliers of goods and services. You have to do your share to be a good customer, because medical care is a partnership. Ever since Dr. Art made it clear that I had some say in my medical treatment, I've always taken ownership of that responsibility.

The next time you need to see a doctor, do your homework first. Come prepared with a written list of symptoms you're experiencing, questions to ask, concerns you have, and medications you're taking. My mother takes a lot of drugs. Interactions between them are always a concern, as is the risk of inadvertently being prescribed two different drugs for the same condition by different doctors. She maintains a written list of everything she takes and gives this list to any new physician she sees. Try to make the doctor's job easier by collaborating in your care decisions. The doctor can do a better job for you with your help.

And isn't it odd that medical care is the one product or service for which it's virtually impossible to get a price quote before you make a purchase decision? And there's no refund policy. Weird.

Chapter 11

OUTSIDE LOOKING IN

Pearl #11: A friend who shares an observation that conflicts with your own self-image provides a great opportunity to better define yourself and how you want to appear to others.

"*O* would some power the giftie gie us to see ourselves as others see us." This famous (if somewhat perplexing) quotation from eighteenth-century Scottish poet Robert Burns expresses the universal desire to know what other people really think of us. Who wouldn't want to be a fly on the wall when you know your friends or family are talking about you? Or to read the secret thoughts in a loved one's diary? Sometimes we are shocked to learn how people feel about us, especially when it conflicts with our own self-perception. Such dissonance suggests that our external behavior isn't consistent with how we really think and feel. Or maybe we just aren't expressing ourselves clearly. So it's a mixed blessing. On the one hand, it's wonderful to learn of complimentary comments surreptitiously. But it can be painful to discover that some people smile to our faces as they criticize us to their friends.

On several occasions, I've learned what someone else really thinks of me. Sometimes this person was someone I cared about who was secretly not happy about something I had said or done. These were certainly upsetting experiences, but they had a benefit. Having that knowledge gave me the opportunity to take corrective action before the relationship suffered irreparable harm. In one case, though, I learned of some negative comments from someone close to me only after that individual had died. Obviously, there was nothing I could do about it at that point except feel guilty (I'm good at that). On the plus side, the insight motivated me to adjust my behavior to try to prevent having other people react to me in the same way.

Every once in a while, a close friend or relative might tell you something about how they perceive you that takes you completely by surprise. When I started graduate school in chemistry, I met another new student named Terry. Terry was 6'5" tall with a big black mustache. Being from Kansas, he walked at a leisurely pace and he drawled a bit when he spoke. Terry was a great guy who became a close friend. You always knew where you stood with Terry; he didn't pull any punches.

One day we were discussing the topic that was forefront in the minds of all the students in our class: who would each of us select as a doctoral thesis advisor? We had all met with the various professors in our department to learn about their research programs and had begun considering the topics we might want to pursue for our doctorates. I was most interested in Professor Smith's work. Terry had not met him yet, so he asked me what Professor Smith was like. "He seems pretty nice," I replied. "He's kind of shy, but I think he'd be a good advisor unless you were really aggressive or something." Terry looked down at me from his lofty perch and said, "You're the most aggressive person I know."

You know that expression "You could have knocked me over with a feather"? It wouldn't have taken much more than a feather to tip me off my feet at that moment. I was absolutely stunned. I had never thought of myself as being aggressive, but obviously I came across that way to my friend Terry. Now, being from Kansas, perhaps Terry was used to easier-going, slower-moving people; any brisk walker and talker like me might have struck him as aggressive. And I wasn't sure exactly what he meant by "aggressive." Was I assertive, abrasive, energetic, combative, contentious, hard-driving, ambitious, or what? There are many interpretations. I didn't know if he was using the term "aggressive" in a pejorative sense. Did he think being aggressive was undesirable, or was he merely using it as a neutral adjective to describe my personality? If I really was aggressive, did that mean I wouldn't be a good fit for Professor Smith's group? Oh my.

Once I began going down this line of thought, more questions came to mind. I contemplated what aspects of my behavior had led Terry to conclude that I was aggressive. I wondered if other people also had interpreted my personality as aggressive or if that was just Terry's perspective.

Next, I asked myself if I agreed that I exhibited those characteristics. I was a fairly bright and motivated graduate student, excited about getting into a research program and accomplishing something. I had done very well academically as an undergraduate and was succeeding in my graduate classes so far. I studied hard and really tried to do a good job. I was moderately competitive, but I also recognized that there were many other smart students there. Maybe these were all signs of being aggressive. I certainly didn't think I was belligerent or hostile. Debating for its own sake had never been my style, nor was getting into other people's faces. Okay, maybe I would agree that I was aggressive in a "Let's kick some chemistry butt!" sense.

I certainly did not wish to be perceived as aggressive in the fashion of trampling on the backs of my peers as I clawed my way to the top. Pushing other people down has never seemed the right way to get ahead. Instead, I've wanted to succeed by learning as much as I can, working hard, and doing an excellent job on whatever I undertake. Some people might consider that as being aggressive. I viewed it as being assertive, ambitious, and goal-oriented: all reasonable qualities in my book. I think—and hope—that's what Terry meant by "aggressive," although he never elaborated.

I had to ask myself if I was comfortable conveying this impression of being aggressive to others. Like most people, I wanted people to like me, but I wasn't inclined to compromise my standards or behavior just to make somebody else happy. If my fellow graduate students saw me as being smart and ambitious, that was all right with me.

As it happened, I did select Professor Smith as my thesis advisor. It was one of the best decisions I ever made. Yes, he was shy and reserved, but he didn't seem to have any problem working with me. He was the best mentor, teacher, guide, and friend a graduate student could hope to have. His quiet exterior belied a core of solid resolve, a brilliant mind, and an exceptional passion for teaching. We got along great, and Professor Smith had a tremendous influence on my life.

Do you think your friends and colleagues see you in the same way you perceive yourself? Or do they observe aspects of your personality that lie in one of your blind spots? Perhaps you have a close friend with whom you can discuss these delicate issues. I'd like the impression I convey to others to be congruent with how I think of myself. That's hard to do if I really don't know how I come across to the rest of the world. It's always enlightening to learn how others perceive you, for better or for worse. Think of it as data that allows you to make an appropriate decision or take an appropriate action. Or not; it's your choice.

When Terry made an offhand comment about his perception of me, I doubt he expected it would lead to an introspection that has lasted close to forty years now. My friend offered me that rare Robert Burns moment: the chance to see myself as at least one other person sees me. The self-analysis that resulted made me more cognizant of how I appear to other people than I ever had been before. I still keep that perspective in mind. Sometimes I care how I'm perceived and other times not so much, but at least I'm more tuned-in to it now.

Chapter 12

JUST A CONTAINER

*Pearl #12: When loved ones pass away, you've just
lost the containers they lived in, not the essence of the
impact they had on family, friends, and community
and not the memories you still hold dear.*

J come from a small family. I'm the oldest of three children. I
had just one aunt, one uncle, and six first cousins, none of
whom I'm in touch with. Because my father was in the military and
we moved frequently, I rarely saw my grandparents or other relatives.
One consequence of growing up in such a small and geographically
distributed family is that we had little experience with death. When my
grandparents, aunt, and uncle died, I was thousands of miles away. I
never had to deal with the illness and passing of one of my older relatives
until my father died just six years ago.

In stark contrast, my wife comes from a huge extended family. Each
of Chris's parents was one of ten children. Most of their descendants

still live within a few miles of the small town in upstate New York where they were born. With a family that large, you get exposed to sickness, old age, death, and funerals from early childhood. It's just part of what people and families go through. It wasn't until I met Chris that I had ever attended a wake and viewed a body in an open casket. I was in my forties before I attended a funeral. Obviously, my experience reflects an extreme insulation from the realities of life's end.

Eight years ago Chris's father passed away. Zeke was a cool guy with many, many friends. He was much beloved in the community where he had lived his entire life. When I first walked into the funeral home and saw Zeke's body lying in his casket, I instantly thought, "That's not Zeke. That's just the container Zeke came in. Zeke's still around here somewhere."

Now, I am not a spiritual person in any way. I do not believe in a spirit or a soul or an afterlife. I do not believe in heaven, hell, purgatory, or reincarnation. I believe I am here now for no particular reason, and I just make the best of it and try to be a net contributor to the health and happiness of people around me in some small way. Still, I found that notion about Zeke and his "container" to be comforting.

In that moment of insight in the funeral home, I realized that the essence of Zeke was neither his physical body, now lifeless but peaceful, nor a mystical soul or spirit that was now residing in some other part of the cosmos or beyond. The essence of Zeke was our memories of him, the influence that he had on his family and friends, the laughter and warmth he brought into the world, the legacy he left through his children, grandchildren, and great-grandchildren. I didn't need to believe that he was "in a better place" to feel consoled. Knowing Zeke for the years that I had and recalling the pleasure of my interactions with him were positive enough feelings.

People hold a wide range of views on death and whatever happens after it. One of my friends has heard the voices of several dead relatives on various occasions, just as if they were speaking to her in life. When she visited the grave of a beloved aunt who had died of leukemia, for instance, she heard her aunt say clearly, "It's okay, honey. I'm in no pain now." Was this the power of suggestion? Wishful thinking? Strong and loving memories of the deceased? Or a true message from beyond? In my view, the reality isn't important if the living find solace from such an encounter.

Another friend had a near-death experience after being electrocuted in a home accident. It was the classic NDE: the tunnel, the white light, the deceased ancestors telling him he had to go back although he wanted to stay, the intense feeling of peace and love. This friend, like me, is non-spiritual, but the episode strongly affected him. He had the distinct sense that one did not have to hold any specific religious beliefs to wind up in that place of love. Regardless of whether such experiences are a function of brain chemistry, ingrained cultural and religious beliefs, or an actual encounter with the afterlife, they are comforting.

Zeke's oldest son delivered a superb eulogy at the funeral. It was heartfelt, loving, contemplative, and funny. He succinctly captured the essence of Zeke's personality and his influence on the people around him. We could all laugh while we cried, remembering the happiness Zeke brought instead of our sadness at his passing. That was Zeke. Not the container, but the memories. I hope I'm able to leave such fond memories when I no longer need the container I walk around in.

Chapter 13

NOW YOU'RE SCARING ME

Pearl #13: It may come as a surprise to realize it,
but the potential for violence lurks inside all of us.

I am not by nature a violent person. I do not typically react to frustration or anger by physically lashing out. I don't throw things across the room, kick the furniture, or slam doors. Nonetheless, I now suspect that, deep down inside, we all have the ability to be violent when pushed to our limits.

I once had a relationship with a woman I'll call Gerri. Gerri was a highly educated and intelligent professional woman I had known years earlier before we reconnected later in life. On the surface, Gerri was sweet and gentle, but underneath that soft exterior lurked demons that I met only later.

Gerri was the only child of a distant father and a mother who had been institutionalized periodically for paranoid schizophrenia. Gerri herself was highly "suspicious" as she put it, frequently distrusting other people's motivations and actions. Even more alarming was her ability to switch from sweetness to rage in an instant. I was also startled by the violent behavior she sometimes exhibited when she was frustrated. Below are a few examples.

Once, when she opened the refrigerator, a plastic bottle of ketchup slipped out of the door and onto her foot. Gerri picked up the bottle and threw it against the kitchen wall as hard as she could. The bottle exploded and spewed ketchup everywhere. The kitchen looked like the set of a Tarantino movie.

I baked her favorite birthday cake, German chocolate, one year. But I got the frosting wrong. I used coconut-almond when I was supposed to use coconut-pecan (or vice versa, who knows). She threw the cake, pan and all, into the driveway for all the neighbors to see.

One evening, Gerri was walking from her car to the front door. Her hands were full, and she dropped her keys. In frustration, she took an empty glass pop bottle she was carrying and smashed it onto the sidewalk.

Gerri thought a young woman in a car had cut her off in a supermarket parking lot. She followed the woman home, got out of her car, and screamed obscenities at her startled victim.

I was not accustomed to seeing this kind of behavior, and I didn't know how to deal with it. Who would? Gerri told me that when she had these episodes, she literally saw red. Surprisingly, none of these actions struck her as being unusual or inappropriate. She was just "high-spirited," she said. I, on the other hand, didn't think this behavior was normal at all.

Not surprisingly, we had some (figuratively speaking) knock-down, drag-out fights during which we shouted accusations and called each other names. This was something I had never done before. Our clashes never escalated to physical contact, but honestly, I was somewhat afraid that she might stab me in my sleep one night. I'll admit I could have been a better partner in our relationship. Her rages and violent reactions seemed disproportionate to my shortcomings, though.

One night, I became so furious during an argument that I stomped my foot on my briefcase, which was lying on the floor in the living room. The innocent briefcase took a fair amount of damage from being caught in the crossfire. I didn't know it was possible for anyone or anything to frustrate or enrage me to the point of violence—even if it was just violence against an inanimate object. I had never lashed out in that way in anger before, and I haven't since.

That brief instant of violent reaction contained a powerful message. It startled me into realizing that I was capable of getting angrier than I believed possible. My brain short-circuited around its usual controls and, unconsciously, my limbs became weapons. For the first time, I understood how people could explode into domestic violence without meaning to. It's never justified, but just then I had a glimpse of how it was possible for an argument to escalate into a violent confrontation.

Obviously, the fight-or-flight survival instinct that's in all of us was alive and well in me. I can imagine situations in which this would be an asset; arguing with your loved ones is not one of them. I hope I never encounter another situation that angers me enough to strike out violently. Should that ever happen, though, I feel confident that I'll be able to channel any necessary violent action for the appropriate purpose of true survival or to protect someone close to me.

In this situation, I eventually opted for the flight option, rather than continue fighting. Gerri and I split up after a few difficult years. The house became calmer after that.

Chapter 14

BEWARE OF GIFTED GEEKS

Pearl #14: Happiness comes from setting realistic expectations for yourself, regardless of what you think the rest of the world demands.

$\mathcal{I}$ was a bit of a contradiction when I was a lad. Like every other member of my immediate family, I was academically gifted. We all did well in school and on aptitude tests. Yet at the same time, for many years, I suffered from a severe inferiority complex. On the one hand, I was proud of my academic ability—maybe too proud—but on the other hand, I acutely felt all my shortcomings and limitations. The negatives generally outweighed the positives. I wasn't very happy.

I'm the oldest child in my family. My parents weren't quite sure how to deal with their gifted children, and I was the first stage of the experiment. They were concerned about keeping my ego in check. They tried assorted techniques. I remember my father telling me, "Just remember, in almost every respect, you're average. You're average looking, you're of average height, you're of average ability." When I was in my early teens, my father once cautioned me, "Whatever you do, someone will be better at it than you are." The obvious corollary to that statement was that someone must be the best at that particular activity; maybe that could be me!

My parents' attempts to control my swelled head through such comments backfired. I overreacted emotionally and concluded that I was well below average in most regards. For many years, I struggled to find an appropriately balanced self-image, acknowledging but not flaunting my strengths and accepting but not dwelling on my limitations.

My quest to overcome my inferiority complex led to a powerful need for external validation of my achievements. That's probably why I have sometimes come across as boastful or arrogant. I really don't mean to. In actuality, I've never felt arrogant at all, and I feel bad if I've conveyed that impression to people.

When I was in my early thirties, a friend offered an exceptional insight on this issue: "You want people to take you seriously, but you're surprised when they do." She hit the nail right on the head. I wanted to achieve something in my life and was energetic in my quest for success, but I found little self-fulfillment from my achievements. Therefore, it was important to have others acknowledge my success. I yearned to have my colleagues and peers value my contributions, yet I was skeptical of their praise. Even today, although I'm proud of my achievements, I don't feel like I do anything that a whole bunch of other people couldn't do. By my definition, if I can do it, it must not be that hard to do.

Such a strong need for external validation really puts you at risk of disappointment if the validation isn't forthcoming. I began speaking at software conferences in early 1991. Before long, I was giving eight or ten conference talks per year. Conference attendees typically complete an evaluation form for each presentation they attend. The conference staff tabulates the results of these evaluations and sends the averages and comments to the speakers. It used to be that when I received my evaluations in the mail, I could feel my pulse shoot up with anxiety. Did the attendees like my talk? Did they like me? Did they find my presentation helpful and my materials professional? I needed to know the truth, but I craved hearing good news. In those days, so much of my ego was tied up with how other people viewed me that I got upset about some of the less-than-stellar evaluations. Who doesn't want to look good in front of their professional peers? I surely did. I still do.

In my early presentations, my slides always received ratings about one full point (out of five) lower than my ratings as a speaker. This data gave me something tangible to work on. I systematically focused on improving the quality of my slides until the ratings were up where I wanted them. This is a good example of how to use such evaluations for a constructive purpose, a data-driven change. But I still became upset if someone made a nasty comment on an evaluation form because I hoped to please everyone.

I don't get upset about those things anymore. I've now delivered well over five hundred keynotes, presentations, and training courses at corporations, conferences, professional society meetings, and so forth. I've seen thousands of evaluation forms and heard thousands of comments from attendees. Long ago, I stopped using the forms in my classes unless the clients requested them, because I know exactly what kind of ratings I'm going to receive. They're going to be very good, and by now it's unlikely I'll see a comment I haven't seen before. People enjoy my presentations. Sure, once in a while there's someone who has a beef with a particular point I made or he didn't like my jokes or he thought the clip art on my slides was corny (it is). Those negative responses don't bother me anymore. The vast majority of audience members rate my presentation skills and materials highly, and I don't sweat the outliers.

Perhaps I've received all the external validation I need to feel confident and fulfilled in my professional career. That's part of it, but I also changed my attitude. I began trying to meet my own standards, not someone else's. My goal is for the attendees at each of my presentations to feel that there was no better way they could have spent that chunk of work time. It's not entirely realistic, but I aim for that and just let it go how it goes.

Consider whose standards you're trying to meet. Do you frequently feel that you fall short of expectations? If so, whose expectations are those? Yours or someone else's? Do you compare yourself to your peers and conclude that you don't measure up in some respect? If so, I offer three suggestions.

First, set your own standards. Strive to make your own expectations of yourself more important to you than what someone else thinks.

Second, look for specific areas where you can improve in a realistic way and to a realistic extent. We can all do better work, have more fun, and be a better person in certain aspects of our lives. In this book, I've described many experiences that helped me on my journey toward these goals. I'm not there yet—I'll never get there—but each day I try to do a bit better than I did the day before. Improving yourself, your work, and your life is a journey, not a destination.

Third, don't worry so much about what other people think of you or about falling short of society's ideal of perfection. Contemporary culture holds up impossible benchmarks of achievement and appearance that only a small fraction of the population can reach. But those are the people who get their pictures in the magazines and the ones who so many others aspire to emulate. You might never look like whomever you think is the most gorgeous actress, and no one will ever confuse me with *People* magazine's sexiest man alive. You're probably never going to win the competition in this week's hottest reality show, and I'm never going to win a Nobel Prize.

We'll live.

Part 3

MOTIVATIONAL PEARLS

I've had some excellent role models in my life who taught me powerful, positive lessons. In this section, I describe several of those messages. My parents, Bud and Ruth Wiegers, feature prominently, as they demonstrated the benefits of continuous learning, the importance of volunteerism, and just how much courage parents can exhibit when their children are threatened. From my parents and others, I learned to respect people who pursue their dreams despite obstacles and to admire people who heroically care for an ailing loved one until they just can't do it anymore on their own.

The examples set by the people in the following stories motivated me to incorporate these values and behaviors into my own life. I hope to emulate these admirable people should I ever find myself in comparable situations. Perhaps these stories will inspire and motivate you to make some positive changes in your own life.

Chapter 15

BECAUSE NO ONE
SHOULD BE HUNGRY

Pearl #15: My father, who sometimes went without food as a child, taught me that no one should ever go hungry and that it's up to all of us to help prevent hunger.

When I was a child, I got into the usual amount of trouble, I suppose. While basically being well behaved, I would sometimes do things I wasn't supposed to do, as all children do. I learned to fear the words, "Wait until your father comes home." (It's the same feeling I would get in the pit of my stomach later in life whenever a significant other would say, "We have to talk.") Not that I had to fear corporal punishment from my father other than the infrequent-but-well-deserved smack on the rear, but I knew there were going to be some consequences.

My father told me long ago that he would never punish his children by sending them to bed without supper. "I know what it's like to be three-days hungry," he said. My father had a terrible childhood. He was raised in a broken home with a succession of stepfathers who would come home drunk and beat him and his mother. I always greatly respected my father for breaking the chain of domestic violence and not propagating it to my generation. But think about that: a child who hasn't eaten for three days in the United States of America, who is not an abandoned orphan or a runaway living on the streets.

I've always felt bad that my father suffered through such an abusive and neglectful childhood. I was proud of him for breaking out of that reality and being successful in whatever he did. (It helped that he was extremely bright and strongly self-motivated.) With those few words, he imparted two important messages to me: food is not a weapon, and every human being should have enough to eat.

When I say I'm hungry, I probably haven't eaten anything for three or four hours. When I say I'm starving, I might have gone six or eight hours without eating. Can you imagine going three days without eating? Neither can I. I've never had to worry about where my next meal is coming from. I've never opened an empty kitchen cabinet or refrigerator and lacked the means to fill it. My brother told me once that when he was off at college with his wife, the contents of their pantry got down to a single can of cherries as they waited for my parents to send them more money. Had I known that earlier, perhaps I could have helped.

There is no excuse for anyone to be hungry in the United States. During tough economic times, many families of limited means have to choose between food and medicine, food and housing, food and the electric bill, food and just about everything else. You can gauge the degree of food insecurity in a community by how many people are getting emergency food boxes from a local food bank. The need is great today in many parts of the country.

My father's words that day in my childhood have stuck with me for my entire life. They motivated my wife and I to become strong financial supporters of Meals on Wheels and the Oregon Food Bank ("... because no one should be hungry" is the slogan for the OFB). For several years, I've participated in volunteer events and helped raise funds for the OFB. At Thanksgiving, Chris and I work through a local women's services organization to donate food for a needy family who are victims of domestic violence. It's the least we can do.

It is one thing to write a check for an organization that helps feed people; it's another to help feed them yourself. In 2008, I decided I should walk my talk. I signed up as a volunteer delivery driver for the Clackamas County Meals on Wheels program. One day a week, I pick up about a dozen meals from a food preparation center and deliver them to senior citizens and people with disabilities who cannot easily get out and shop for themselves.

The clients on my route have become friends I enjoy seeing each week. Some of them have introduced me to their pets and children. One eighty-nine-year-old World War II veteran, a former Marine aviator, chats with me about our mutual interest in airplanes, lends me aviation books, and shares the occasional bawdy joke. Some of my clients are in wheelchairs, some are blind or have other disabilities, and some are just old and not very mobile.

I've seen my clients get sick or injured and then recover. Several people have dropped off my route because they moved into a nursing home or passed away. When clients cancel their delivery for the day— or forever—I worry about them and hope they're doing okay. I've sympathized with my clients when they have lost a spouse after more than sixty years of marriage. One day I had to call the paramedics when a client experienced a seizure just as I handed him his meal. Food flew everywhere as he collapsed on the floor. Fortunately, he was okay, but that was an eventful day on the Meals route.

At fifty-seven, I'm one of the younger drivers at my Meals on Wheels center. We have drivers in their seventies and eighties who are in good health and donate their time to help their less fortunate peers. We all find it satisfying to provide people with nutritious meals they might not otherwise have. I walk away from each door pleased that I can help someone stay in his or her own home and continue to live independently. I know my clients genuinely appreciate the meal delivery service, as well as a brief visit from a friendly face each weekday.

I encourage you to look for ways to help alleviate hunger in your community. Food pantries, food banks, and meal programs always need volunteers, food, and donations. When I've asked people at the OFB how I could do the most good, they said frankly, "Give money." They have the ability to amplify donations through their purchasing arrangements. So instead of giving them ten dollars' worth of food, I give them ten dollars in cash, which they can use to buy several times as much food. All it really takes to motivate you to become a Meals on Wheels driver is to imagine that it's your own parent who doesn't have access to even one substantial, balanced meal a day.

An even more personal way to contribute to curing hunger is to feed one person in need. Portland, like many other cities, has swarms of panhandlers looking for handouts on downtown streets or carrying crudely lettered cardboard signs by freeway exit ramps. I'm sure many of these people are legitimately needy. Unfortunately, some of them are not—they do this for a living. It's frustrating because you can't distinguish the people who really are hungry and homeless from those on the make. I won't give money to panhandlers anymore, but I have sometimes given one some food.

One Saturday Chris and I stopped at our favorite bagel place for lunch. Driving out of the parking lot, we saw a young man carrying a backpack and a "homeless and hungry" sign. That was an odd place to see someone with such a sign. He looked legitimate. I turned the car around, stopped, and got his story. He was nineteen and on his own, and he really was in dire straits. We took him back to the bagel shop where we bought him lunch and some extra food as well. The shop owner also made a generous contribution. So at least that young man had a full stomach for a couple of days.

Like me, my friend Norm won't give cash to people looking for a handout. But once he did offer to buy a homeless man some food. The two of them walked into a grocery store in downtown Boston, and Norm paid for whatever the man wanted. When he walked out of the store, the man handed most of the food to one of his homeless friends and said, "Pass it around." Maybe several hungry people ate well that day. Shouldn't everyone?

Chapter 16

FOR WHOM THE
SCHOOL BELL TOLLS

*Pearl #16: Pursuing education as an adult can lead to a
more rewarding career and a more fulfilling personal life.*

*M*y friend Lea just completed the final course for her bachelor's degree in archaeology. Lea is thirty-five years old. She's been going to college full-time for the past four years while working one, and sometimes two, low-paying part-time jobs. Lea is bright, motivated, and energetic, but for various reasons she didn't go to college right out of high school. I'm proud of Lea and impressed with her dedication and commitment to pursuing her education and a more fulfilling career.

I've always been impressed with adults who go back to college when they have many distractions and responsibilities. My mother graduated from Boise State College the year before I did and placed very high in her class. My father received his bachelor's degree from the same college a few years later. I was proud of both of them.

Many of my coworkers at Kodak attended college at night while working full-time during the day. Some obtained bachelor's degrees so they could advance from a technician-level job to a professional-level position. Others pursued master's degrees in computer science or software engineering so they could enhance their professional qualifications and perform better on their assignments. One research technician eventually completed a doctorate in polymer science and became a professional research chemist.

One former colleague, Bruce, completed master's degrees in both computer science and computer engineering through a university's distance learning program when he was in his forties. He was just a sponge for knowledge. It was no coincidence that he was also one of the best software developers I've ever known. The university finally forced Bruce to graduate with his second master's degree because he had so many credits. These people all demonstrated inspiring commitment, dedication, and sacrifice in their quests for knowledge.

My wife also pursued the adult education pathway. As a teenager, Chris aspired to become a teacher. Financial limitations led her to get a two-year degree instead, and she spent the next twenty-six years working as a secretary. She was an outstanding secretary, but she still wanted to teach. In 1997, Chris left Kodak after twenty-five years and enrolled in a one-year early childhood education program at her local community college.

You should have seen Chris on her first day of school that fall. She climbed onto that big yellow school bus, a pink bow in her hair, with sharpened pencils and new notebooks in her sturdy leather satchel, eager to learn and make new friends. I exaggerate only slightly. As I watched Chris leave for her first day of classes, I remembered that feeling, the excitement and anticipation of learning about the world and charting a course toward the rest of my life.

By her second semester, some of the thrill was gone. Chris stuck it out, though, and sure enough, by June she was a preschool teacher. I was proud of her for leaving the security of a long-time corporate job and pursuing what she had always wanted to do. She discovered soon that many of the skills she used at Kodak transferred to the preschool classroom. Dealing with three-year-olds is pretty much like dealing with PhD scientists, except that you can reason with three-year-olds.

Recently, Chris extended her interests to writing clever and engaging short stories. She has taken several writing classes at local colleges and attended an annual writer's conference here in Portland. The structure of a formal class helps many people acquire new knowledge in a systematic way. Interactions with instructors and fellow students also enrich the learning environment. The students in adult education classes are more motivated than your typical twenty-year-old college classmate. The adults are all there because of their passion for the subject or because they really want to complete their degrees to change careers.

You don't need a nearby university and an intended career path to keep learning. My friend Sue, a retired high school and college Spanish teacher, began taking French lessons from a local continuing education resource. She travels a great deal, so the French doubtless will come in handy someday. I think Sue would always be taking a class even if she didn't have an explicit plan to use the knowledge. That's just the way she is. Sue has passed on her passion for learning to her nine-year-old granddaughter, who attends a Japanese language immersion school, takes Spanish and guitar lessons, knits, sews, does origami, and attended a rock-and-roll camp for girls. Whew!

I have other friends with insatiable appetites for knowledge. They never cease to impress me. One is a master craftsman who studies woodworking magazines and takes classes in metalworking. He has also been taking drum lessons for decades, on top of working as an electrical engineer, software developer, and consultant throughout his career. Just the thought of cramming all that knowledge into my brain makes me feel top-heavy. Two other friends, one in his late fifties, recently learned to fly airplanes, which is no trivial undertaking.

Even if you're on a time or monetary budget, learning opportunities abound. Two years ago my sister decided to refurbish most of her house. At the time, she knew nothing about home renovation. As Kathy told me, "Thanks to some classes at the local home-improvement megastore, reading a ton of books, watching someone else do it, and just screwing things up, I've learned more about home renovation in the last two years than I have on any topic since college." The Internet provides limitless options for free or low-cost education on any topic you can imagine. You just have to take advantage of these opportunities and launch your quest for knowledge.

Learning is good for you. It stimulates your brain, which might help stave off mental deterioration, particularly if you are learning about a domain that is completely new to you. It stimulates your soul by keeping you engaged with the world and the people in it. As Sue put it, "I love taking classes for two reasons: one is to learn and the other is social. I meet fabulous people, make connections, and learn from them, thereby expanding my knowledge and network."

A love of learning and a commitment to lifelong education is a wonderful value to pass along to your children. My family was always intellectually curious when I was growing up. We played a lot of games, and we all read a lot. I have no children, but my brother and sister bequeathed the value of knowledge to their children. My brother's daughter received a doctorate in applied mathematics; his son obtained a master's in mechanical engineering.

Projects that don't go entirely as planned provide excellent learning opportunities. Whether it was an assignment at work or just an activity around the house, a project gone awry presents the opportunity to do a better job the next time. A completely successful project doesn't offer nearly as many lessons learned. The success might even make you overconfident. You might think you can repeat the success on the next project even if it is a lot bigger and more complex. It's not fun to have things go wrong, but doing a little retrospective thinking helps you make lemonade from the lemons.

I sometimes feel guilty that I haven't acquired more formal education and attended more classes just for fun and life enrichment. The various wine-tasting classes I've taken were informative and great fun, but that's sort of a special case. I would be a much better musician today had I systematically taken guitar lessons for the past forty-four years rather than just taking them occasionally when I wanted to learn a new playing style. I do read a variety of books and magazines, so I pick up a diversity of knowledge that way. The love of knowledge and a passion for learning are embedded in me even if I've only occasionally pursued it in a formal way.

Think about what you have always wanted to learn. Where can you take a class or some lessons? Most towns offer a wide variety of educational opportunities at community colleges, high schools, museums, and community centers. Don't wait until you're all caught up on everything else in your life so you can finally sign up for that creative writing class or join that reading group. I learned long ago that you never get caught up on life. You just need to make the time for your top priorities, and that includes enriching your own brain.

I take my hat off to all those adults who have made the commitment and sacrifice to pursue higher education while still keeping the lawn mowed, the house clean, and the family fed. Way to go, Chris, Bud, Ruth, Mike T., Mike M., Bruce, Tom, Lea, Norm, and all the others! I salute you.

Chapter 17

LENDING A HAND

Pearl #17: Everyone should look for opportunities to help people in need because even a small contribution can have a great impact on the lives of others.

My parents both set an excellent example for me through the volunteer work they did. My father retired from the Air Force at age thirty-six and then spent nearly twenty years working in private industry before retiring for good. After retiring, he contributed thousands of hours of volunteer work to the Idaho State Library. When he hit the three-thousand-hour mark, the staff led a kazoo parade throughout the library to celebrate.

My mother was no slouch either when it came to volunteering and community service. She was active in a parent education center, in Head Start preschool programs, in a group of parents and youths fighting drug abuse, and in parent-teacher organizations. She tutored foster teenagers and worked with the parents of gifted and talented children. My mother received several awards for her volunteerism. *The Idaho Statesman* newspaper named her an Idaho Distinguished Citizen, and she was invited to carry the Olympic torch as it passed through Boise in 2002. I didn't realize that each of the thousands of runners in the Olympic torch relay carries a different torch, which is used to light the next torch in the series. Each participant has the opportunity to purchase the torch she carried during her leg of the relay. The torch my mother carried still occupies a place of honor in her apartment.

Because of my parents' commitment to helping others, they served as admirable role models for the rest of my family. My brother, Bruce, and my sister, Kathy, have also spent considerable time volunteering, much of it for the Boy Scouts and Girl Scouts. What could be more relaxing than a sleepover with nine hundred Girl Scouts at a football stadium? Long after their own children were grown, Bruce and his wife, Robin, foster-parented three young children. I've always respected their decision to bring three kids with special needs into their lives and into their home.

My siblings bequeathed the importance of volunteering to their own children. Kathy volunteered with her two young daughters at a local animal shelter. She can tell you how it feels to be dragged down the street at ninety miles per hour by an enthusiastic pit bull. My niece Brandy devoted a lot of energy to the Girl Scouts, even when she was studying for her PhD and afterward. Partly as a consequence of her volunteer work, Brandy also was invited to carry the torch for the 2002 Olympic Games. How exciting it was for a grandmother and granddaughter to share such an extraordinary experience!

I've tried to carry on my parents' personal ethic of volunteerism, and volunteer work has become more important to me as I've gotten older. Like my father, I have volunteered at public libraries for many years. Chris and I volunteer at our local branch two mornings a week. If someone in Clackamas County requests a library item that happens to reside in our collection, we're the people who take it from the shelves and route it to the customer's local library. We also help out with the library's used book sales. The main drawback is that we take home way too many of the books ourselves; our backlog reading piles are out of control. I've also done volunteer work for Meals on Wheels, the Oregon Food Bank, and other food-related causes. I find these activities rewarding because it feels good to help other people.

Communities always need volunteers. You can get involved with school activities, youth groups, senior citizen centers, the Red Cross, volunteer firefighter and ambulance crews, church groups, Neighborhood Watch, fundraising events, and nonprofit organizations of all kinds. The list is endless. Sadly, so is the need.

Through some of my activities, I've met people who just live to volunteer. One young woman I met attends a university several hours from her home in Portland. Whenever she is back in the city, she tries to find a volunteer opportunity. One of my retired friends has volunteered as the treasurer for several nonprofit organizations. He recently became the treasurer for an organization dedicated to stopping war. There are few nobler—or more challenging—causes than that.

Many high schools now require students to complete a community volunteer project before they graduate. This is a fine idea. You don't need to do much to help someone less fortunate. It's good to learn that at an early age.

There are many ways to assist your fellow man other than through formal volunteering. You can help others as you go about your daily life. When I spot someone with a problem, my instinct is to see if I can lend a hand. Being a motorcyclist myself, I've given a couple of stranded riders a lift when their bike failed them, once in my car and once on my bike. When I've seen someone being sick at the side of the road, I've stopped to see if he required assistance. Many people will drive right by, oblivious to the possibility that someone whose path they've crossed could use their help. It doesn't take much time or effort to stop, and your involvement could make a big difference.

When we lived in Rochester, New York, Chris and I drove to Niagara Falls one December evening to see the colored holiday lights playing on the falls. It was spectacular. On our way home on the New York State Thruway, I saw a man at the side of the road next to a stopped car, frantically waving his arms. I pulled over to the shoulder. Chris looked at me in surprise. We've all heard horror stories of Good Samaritans who stopped to help a stranded motorist, only to be robbed, carjacked, or worse. But I really didn't think that someone wanting to entrap a victim for nefarious purposes would try to do so by standing on the Thruway in the ten-degree cold at night.

The man said that he was in the process of moving to Virginia with his wife and infant daughter. His car had stalled. No one else had stopped when he tried to flag them down. Sure enough, a woman in a big coat was huddled in the car holding a baby. How can you not help people stuck in such a frightening and dangerous situation? I led the mother and her baby back to my car to stay warm. Her husband and I hooked up jumper cables and got their car started. Chris and I drove on down the road, but I've always felt guilty that I didn't stay to make sure they were able to get moving. I've stopped to offer assistance to drivers at the side of the road on several other occasions. Sometimes they were okay. In one case I helped someone deal with a car problem; in another it was emotional difficulties that led a distraught woman to pull over at a freeway exit ramp. A little comforting helped her get back on the road.

The next time you spot somebody who looks like they might be in a jam, consider stopping to help if it looks like a safe thing to do. At least you can call AAA or the police, ambulance, or fire department for assistance. If you ever find yourself in a similar situation, you'll certainly be grateful for anyone who lends you a hand. One time my wife's car wouldn't start while she was visiting a friend. Fortunately, a considerate neighbor came out to jump-start her car. The next day I bought a new battery. When a car battery begins to fail, it goes fast.

We'll all come out ahead if each of us looks for opportunities to contribute to the health and well-being of our fellow man. Look around your neighborhood. Perhaps there's a senior citizen living nearby who could use some help with home repairs or sprucing up her yard. You might spot some parks, rivers, beaches, or streets that need to be cleaned up. Once or twice a year I walk down the hill I live on and pick up litter from the sides of the road. Look around your community. Are there hungry people you can help feed, foster children who lack school supplies or winter clothing, or other kids who could use a reading tutor? The volunteer possibilities are endless. It takes just a little effort to help out; it means an awful lot.

Chapter 18

RACING FOR YOUR DREAMS

Pearl #18: It's never too late to pursue your childhood dreams.

My father, Bud, loved automobile racing. He attended auto races when he was growing up in Denver and dreamed of becoming a race car driver someday. When our family moved to Boise in 1965, we began attending the Saturday night races at the short track in the small nearby town of Meridian. Several classes of modified and stock cars raced at the Meridian Speedway back then.

It wasn't long before Dad decided to follow his dream. He had a race car built in the C class, the slowest of the three modified classes. It wasn't a very pretty car, tall and ungainly, but now Bud was a race car driver! Next he needed a pit crew. That would be me. You weren't supposed to be able to get into the pits until you were at least sixteen for insurance reasons. I was only fourteen, but I was tall, so we pulled it off. Not that I knew what I was doing, but sometimes Dad just needed another pair of hands to get things done with the car.

Then came the big day: his very first race at the ripe old age of thirty-eight. He made it three-quarters of the way around the track and spun out on the first lap. The transmission in his car was tricky. He operated the clutch by hand using a long lever on the outside of the car. For some reason, the car builder had mounted two separate shift handles on the transmission, each controlling two of the gears. Dad somehow managed to get the car stuck in two gears at once as he was trying to get it moving after the spin. The car had to be towed back to the pits so he could fix the transmission. It was kind of embarrassing, but these things happen. Fortunately, only a few thousand people were watching.

Future races went better, and he did have a good time driving. After a couple of years without much success, though, he decided to sell the car to a friend, who modified it and did much better on the track. Our family was still bitten by the racing bug, though. When I was sixteen, Dad bought a stock car from one of the other drivers and invited me to drive it. Okaaaaayyyy. Despite being termed a "stock car," my 1958 Ford didn't much resemble the way it had come from the dealer twelve years earlier. It had big racing slicks for tires, a full roll cage, no glass, and a high-compression racing engine. I still didn't know what I was doing, but hey, I was a race car driver!

My previous "racing" experience consisted only of putting a few rather slow laps on my father's car on an otherwise empty track. Fortune did not favor me that year, I'm afraid. A young woman in the racing auxiliary group wrote a short blurb about a selected driver each week for the racing program. When she chose me, I was described as "hard-charging rookie driver Karl Wiegers" (all drivers were either hard-charging or lead-footed). What this really meant was that I kept charging into hard things, which wasn't very good for the car. I only had one significant wreck that year, but then the engine blew up and we never really got back on track.

The next year I did better, even winning one heat race. Then one night another car spun me out going into turn three. It was a peculiar sensation to be speeding forward one second and, an instant later, to be going the exact opposite direction with all the other cars heading right toward me, one of them embedded in my left front fender. Traveling backwards at about forty miles per hour, I slammed into the retaining wall. The wreck crumpled up the rear end of the car like an accordion, broke the motor mounts, jammed the drive shaft into the transmission, and terminated my racing career.

My father soldiered on in the racing business. He had already been a driver, pit man, and car owner. Next he became the president of the Meridian Racing Association. In 1970, he conceived, wrote, and published the first and only racing association yearbook. It had pictures and biographies of all the drivers (including yours truly) and details of every race that year, amply illustrated with action photographs. He was also the speedway's promoter for several years, arranging special events, printing posters, and publicizing upcoming races. He moved on to being the track announcer. Maybe Bud wasn't driving a car anymore, but boy was he involved with racing and having the time of his life.

There were still more positions to fill, though. Later he served as the pit steward, who was responsible for all the activities taking place in that mysterious behind-the-scenes area known as the pits. Ultimately he became the track flagman. In his black-and-white striped shirt, Dad made sure the cars were lined up properly and waved the green flag to launch them into competition. As the cars roared by lap after lap, he would wave the yellow caution flag when there was a wreck, the white flag when there was just one lap to go, and the checkered flag as the winner crossed the finish line. There was nothing Bud didn't do at the Meridian Speedway except sell concessions.

I went off to graduate school in the fall of 1973 and left racing behind, although I still enjoy watching car races on television. The next summer I received a call from my mother. "Your father's been in an accident at the speedway," she began. "Is he dead?" I asked. "No," she replied, "but he's in pretty bad shape." The next day I flew from Illinois back to Boise. Dad was indeed in bad shape.

Historically at the Meridian Speedway, the flagman would begin each race by standing on the edge of the infield and waving the green flag. After the double line of cars whizzed by, he would run across the track, jump onto the flag stand just above the concrete crash wall, and continue flagging the race from there. On the night of Dad's accident, a car came onto the track to join the race after he'd waved the green flag. Dad did not see the late car coming as he crossed the track. It slammed right into him.

The crowd gasped in horror as Dad flew through the air and smacked onto the hard asphalt. My younger brother, Bruce, was sitting in his race car in the pits, waiting to compete in the next race. (His racing career was far more successful than either Dad's or mine.) Bruce's pit man ran to him, shouting, "Your dad's been in an accident! I think he might have been killed!" Bruce scrambled out of his car and ran over to see what had happened.

Dad was alive but badly injured. His right collarbone was broken. He had assorted abrasions from the asphalt and possibly some internal injuries. His left arm suffered the most severe damage. The upper arm bone was fractured, and both of his lower arm bones were pulverized, white bone protruding through the skin. After several hours of surgery, he had a lot of metal in that arm holding the bone fragments together and a massive cast.

Dad came home in a few days and slept in a hospital bed in the living room. As he gradually healed, he began a grueling physical therapy program to restore as much strength and motion as possible in the shattered arm. Eventually Dad regained full use of his arm, although he sure had an impressive collection of scars. Mostly he was looking forward to setting off the metal detector at the airport the next time he flew, but the titanium plates and pins didn't trigger the detector. He was disappointed.

That was the end of my father's hands-on involvement with the Meridian Speedway. He continued to attend the races there for years, and he also became a devoted fan of NASCAR and Indy car racing. Both of my parents were present at Phoenix International Raceway when Tom Cruise filmed parts of *Days of Thunder*, a movie about NASCAR.

A man who had always loved racing and dreamed of being behind the wheel had done everything there was to do at the local track. He showed leadership and initiative in chasing the dream of his lifetime. You've got to respect someone who pursues a childhood goal with such dedication.

What are your dreams, both personal and professional? Do you wistfully think "Maybe someday ..." or are you pursuing your dreams now? Are you working at the job you really want to have, or are you just putting food on the table? My friend Eric sold the biochemistry business he had built up and spent the next few years touring wine areas around the world with his wife. Then he opened a great wine shop called Wine Xing ("Wine Crossing"). Another friend began baking gluten-free nutrition bars to keep her fueled on her hikes, bicycle rides, and rock-climbing expeditions. Now you can buy delicious Wild Alice Bars in many stores in the Northwest.

Perhaps you see too many obstacles that are stopping you from chasing your dream. There are always plenty of reasons—I mean excuses—for sticking with the status quo and staying in your comfort zone. But the dream won't come to you: you have to go after it. It's never too late. Maybe you can start today.

Chapter 19

THE BRAVEST THING I EVER SAW

Pearl #19: People can demonstrate extraordinary
courage when confronted with a life-threatening situation.

*Y*ou don't want to go through a house fire. It's a terrible and terrifying event. My family had the bad luck to experience such a fire. The best aspect of the experience was that we all survived with no injuries. The only other good thing that came out of it was the opportunity to watch my parents do the bravest thing I ever saw.

When I was almost ten years old, my father was transferred from Étain-Rouvres Air Base in northeastern France to Mountain Home Air Force Base, Idaho. Étain, where we had been living for about a year, is a village near Verdun, a city that was at the center of one of the longest and most horrific battles of World War I. The French and German armies fought at a stalemate in trench warfare for most of 1916, resulting in more than two hundred and fifty thousand dead and nearly twice that number wounded. Verdun was a fascinating place to live from a historical perspective. We saw many reminders of World War I in the region, including old, partially filled-in trenches next to our housing area (what civilians call a subdivision). We couldn't play there because the trenches still contained unexploded weaponry.

One day we returned from a vacation to a sign on our door that read: MOUNTAIN HOME, IDAHO. Apparently, this was the Air Force's way of notifying my father of his next assigned post. Within a few weeks, we had packed up and moved to Idaho, a state we knew nothing about. We took the SS *America* ocean liner across the Atlantic from Le Havre, France. That was a thrill for all of us. We picked up our Opel station wagon after docking in New York City and drove clear across the country. After living in Europe for three years, I was fascinated that we didn't have to go through customs whenever we crossed the border into another state. Television was an exciting revelation also. We hadn't seen any TV since my mother accidentally fried our set in Italy by forgetting to plug it into the 230-to-120 volt transformer first.

Our destination was smack dab in the middle of the Idaho desert. Upon arriving, we learned that our base housing was not yet available. We had to live for a few weeks in a small mobile home in the town of Mountain Home, ten miles from the air base. The mobile home had a small kitchen and an eating and sleeping area in the front next to an outside door. A narrow passageway led past a heating unit and bathroom to the back part of the trailer, which contained two bedrooms and a second outside door. My parents slept in the front part of the trailer; my brother, sister, and I slept in the back.

One night while we all were sleeping, my mother woke up about midnight. She was horrified to see flames running the full width of the trailer near the ceiling, along the top of the kitchen cabinets in that front compartment. Mom woke up my father. They had no idea what the conditions were in the back of the trailer where we children were sleeping. For all they knew, that part of the trailer was an inferno and we were all dead. They knew we weren't strong enough to open the back door to escape because it was jammed, thanks to the trailer resting askew on its blocks.

With no hesitation or concern for their own safety, my parents ran down that narrow passageway, through the flames, past the malfunctioning heater that had caused the fire, to the back of the trailer. Mom told me later that the thought, "You're going to get burned," flashed into her mind, but that didn't slow her down. Parents react instinctively when their children are threatened. I didn't realize there was a problem until my parents woke up the three of us. They immediately kicked the jammed door open, and all five of us got out, frightened but unharmed.

My father ran back through the trailer's front door a few times to grab armfuls of clothing and other items. This was brave of him but probably not the smartest move, considering that the propane tank on the front of the trailer could have exploded at any moment. We woke up the caretakers of the trailer park, who lived in the one actual house on the lot, and they called the fire department.

I remember watching the trailer burn while waiting for the firefighters to arrive. Solid columns of flames roared out of both doors and shot dozens of feet into the night sky as the fire consumed the trailer. It took the fire department an inordinate amount of time to arrive. Mountain Home was a town of just ten thousand people with only two trailer parks. And yet somehow the firemen went to the wrong trailer park. By the time they finally arrived and extinguished the blaze, there was nothing left of the trailer but a shell.

The next few days were a blur. Neighbors lent us clothing. We stayed in temporary quarters on the base until we could move into our assigned housing. My father salvaged a few repairable items from the ashes. But we lost a lot of mementos from the three years we had spent living in Italy and France and sightseeing throughout Europe. You just can't replace carefully edited home movies of your children playing in the Roman Colosseum. You can't replace our green felt Bavarian hats studded with souvenir pins from all the places we visited in Europe.

You know what, though? That's just stuff. Memories are more important than memorabilia. I still have the memories of the fascinating things we saw during our three years in Europe. You can always get more stuff, even if it's not exactly the same. Nobody was hurt in the fire, which was a miracle. That's a lot more important than losing some of your stuff.

Thank goodness for my mom's extra senses, the ones that woke her up while the rest of us slumbered on. And thank goodness for the incredible courage my parents showed by dashing directly into a wall of fire to rescue us three children. I hope I'm never in a position where I have to make the same kind of snap decision. If I am, though, I hope I will be able to show the same bravery and heroism my mother and father did that terrible night.

Chapter 20

DO ALL YOU CAN,
THEN GET HELP

*Pearl #20: There is no shame in requesting
assistance when you've reached the limits of
what you can do in a difficult situation.*

My father got sick in August of 2004 when he was seventy-five. He had been experiencing some cognitive and physical problems, so he went to see a neurologist. CT scans revealed three lesions in his brain that were most likely malignant tumors. Without drilling into Dad's brain and doing a biopsy to see exactly what these lesions were, it was hard for his doctor to know what kind of treatment to provide. The prognosis for such conditions at his age was not encouraging. My father opted for no biopsy and no treatment. "I'm seventy-five years old," he said. "I've had a good life." No one in our family argued with him about his choice to let nature take its course, although certainly we were all hoping that the situation was not as dire as it appeared.

Nature did take its course; it wasn't pretty. The immediate family—my two siblings and I, our spouses, and my nieces and nephew—convened at the family home in Boise on Labor Day weekend. The problems my father was experiencing were evident to all of us at that point. He had trouble finding words and completing sentences, which frustrated him terribly. He seemed overwhelmed by the presence of so many people in his house and the associated hubbub. I think he just wanted to be left alone. Over the next several weeks, the brain tumors continued to grow. Dad experienced more and more problems with walking and balance, and his speech, understanding, and judgment continued to deteriorate. Brain cancer is not a nice way to die.

Dad remained at home as he got sicker. My mother cared for him to the best of her ability. She really was heroic. Despite her own physical limitations and pains, she devoted all of her energy to keeping Dad comfortable and happy. One time when he lost his balance and fell, she tried to catch him but strained her own hip in the process. The washing machine was running almost constantly as she tried to keep him in clean pajamas after he became confused about where the bathroom was. Poor Dad knew that he wasn't working right and that he was imposing a burden on her, but there was nothing he or anyone else could do. Other members of the family helped out as best they could. The onus was really on my mother, though.

Eventually, it became clear that Mom could no longer take care of Dad at home by herself. With considerable reluctance, she decided that Dad needed professional care in a safe environment. She looked into various options and decided to take advantage of the hospice service provided by the Veterans Administration Medical Center in Boise.

She felt guilty about this decision, but the rest of the family all supported her. We knew it was the only sensible thing to do. Dad was going to die soon no matter what anyone did. We didn't want our mother suffering along with our father any more than necessary.

She did all anyone could have done to take care of her husband of fifty-five years.

My mother was always a deeply nurturing caregiver. I have this theory that, whenever you're sick or hurt or scared, no matter how old or mature you are, you want your mom, and any mom-type person will do. My mom is that kind of a mom, the one you want to have around when all is not well. She took care of everybody in the family and did a terrific job, but even she had limits. She simply could not monitor my father twenty-four hours a day to make sure that he didn't wander around the house and fall down the stairs in the middle of the night, accidentally set the house on fire, or have some other accident.

One Saturday the time had come. My brother, my mother, and I took Dad to the VA Medical Center. The staff there did a fine job. They kept him safe and comfortable, and they treated him with respect. Hospice care really is a civilized way to end your natural life with dignity. Within a couple of weeks, just two months after his diagnosis, Dad passed away. He had a funeral with full military honors, which he earned for his twenty years of Air Force service.

I think my mother feels like she didn't do enough to take care of Dad. That's not the case, though. She did everything anyone in her position could have done and more. It's really hard when we have to acknowledge our limitations and solicit professional assistance, hiring strangers to do something that we thought was our responsibility. You never know when the right time is to make such a change. You never know if you're making the right decision. No magic little green light comes on that says, "Call the VA today." You just make the best guess you can with the available information. Feeling guilty about it doesn't accomplish anything, although it's a natural reaction to making such a difficult and uncertain decision. Everyone in our family was grateful to Mom for her devoted efforts. No one thought any less of her for concluding that it was time for hospice to take over Dad's care.

Through my Meals on Wheels volunteering, I've met a number of senior citizens, many in their eighties and some in their nineties. Two men on my route, Bob and Paul, were upset when their wives had to move into care facilities, one because of Alzheimer's disease and the other due to Parkinson's. Periodically, I would ask them how their wives were doing. I could see the sadness in their eyes and hear the catch in their voices. Eventually Bob's wife passed away. Paul's wife is still in the Alzheimer's facility. Paul visits her there several times a week. He tells me that she always says, "I want to come home." Paul also wants her to come home, of course, but she probably never will. He did the best he could to take care of her. Then he needed some help too. That's just the way it goes.

These decisions are terribly hard. There often is no silver lining. Knowing our limits is the kindest thing we can do for ourselves and, ultimately, for our loved ones in need, because this will result in the person getting the best care in the end. You're not abdicating your responsibilities if you ask for help. Instead, you're fulfilling your responsibilities by arranging for the care your loved one really needs when you just can't do it yourself anymore.

Part 4

PRACTICAL PEARLS

By nature, I'm a pragmatist, not a theorist or an idealist. I'm interested in practical techniques for getting my work done faster and more accurately. I'm always looking for ways to meander through life more easily and more securely.

The practical insights I present in this section continue to be useful in my daily life, and I hope they will be useful to you too. Some of the lessons help me make better product choices, deal with the world as it really is (instead of how I might like it to be), and avoid disappointment, frustration, and even serious personal harm. Other lessons illustrate how frequently you can negotiate with merchants or problematic neighbors to your benefit and how little extra effort it often takes to do a high-quality job instead of a mediocre one.

Chapter 21

THINK FIRST, BUY LATER

*Pearl #21: Carefully consider the features and
characteristics you really want in a product you
buy before you hand over your money.*

few years ago I needed a new clock radio with an alarm. I
went to my local department store and picked out one that
seemed appropriate. That night I went to set the alarm for the first time.
I was annoyed to see that no little red light came on to show me that
the alarm was enabled. Most clock radios I've used have lights to show
a.m. versus p.m. and to indicate whether the alarm is set. The only way I
could tell if this alarm was set was by looking at the switch on the top of
the unit. I've learned how to judge the position of that switch by feel in
the dark. However, it's always more comforting to see the little glowing
light that means I'm going to wake up when I want to.

I have no one but myself to blame for this silly clock radio. I didn't
think carefully about my requirements before I got out my credit card.

I should have taken a few moments to think about what features are important to me in a clock radio. I might have been able to find exactly the kind of unit I was looking for, even if it cost a bit more than the one I bought.

It's kind of embarrassing to admit that I didn't think about my requirements for the clock radio. I've spent much of the past fifteen years writing about, speaking about, and helping companies improve how they handle the requirements for their software projects. I guess I thought a modest, everyday purchase didn't warrant contemplating requirements, but of course it does. Why should I waste even ten dollars on a purchase I'll regret if a few moments of thought will lead me to a more satisfactory choice?

Skimping on requirements analysis for a minor purchase is one thing. It's a really bad idea when making a larger investment. Years ago I carpooled with a man named Pierre. One day Pierre picked me up in his new car. He complained that he had trouble seeing out of the rear window when he was backing up. "Didn't you notice this problem when you test-drove the car?" I asked. He admitted, slightly embarrassed, "Oh, I never drove the car before I bought it."

I was astonished. If I'm spending multiple thousands of dollars on a product, I think long and hard about what I want. I research the various alternatives, read reviews, and get as much information as I can find. I try out the product if I can. If I'm buying a vehicle, I'll take it for a couple of substantial test drives. Only then might I write a check with a comma in it. This strategy helps me avoid unpleasant surprises and buyer's remorse.

I now try to contemplate my real needs before I buy anything that I expect to use for years—whether it's an expensive item or not. Someday I will need a new blow-dryer for my hair. I like the one I have, but naturally this model will no longer be available by the time mine dies. Last month I stayed at a hotel that provided a blow-dryer in the bathroom. It had a single switch with four defined positions: off, low heat and low fan, low heat and high fan, high heat and high fan. I prefer to have separate heat and fan switches so I can get more combinations to help make my hair look beautiful. Moreover, the switch was positioned on the handgrip such that I inadvertently changed the setting multiple times while using the dryer. If I had bought one of these blow-dryers without thinking about such factors, I would've been really irritated. I probably would have tossed it out within a week and bought something different.

I'm pretty good about defining my requirements when buying something big like a car or a house. I use checklists and rating sheets to help me identify the products that best fit my needs. I identify characteristics I wish to avoid as well as those I desire. One negative feature can outweigh five positive ones when it comes to user satisfaction.

Naturally, there's an emotional component as well, but I try not to let my emotions stop me from first thinking about what I'm really looking for. In other words, I'm not an impulse buyer when it comes to big purchases that aren't easy to undo. I've known too many people who bought something shiny just because it caught their eye and regretted it once they encountered the product's shortcomings.

This systematic strategy works. Eleven years ago my wife and I came to Portland on a house-hunting trip. We had one week to buy a house. If we didn't find a satisfactory house, we would rent until we could shop more leisurely, but we wanted to avoid having to move twice if possible. In two-and-a-half days we looked at twenty-eight homes with the help of a good real estate agent. Chris and I each carried a clipboard with rating sheets so we could evaluate each house in numerous dimensions. Fortunately, we have similar tastes in houses and furniture, and we knew just what we were looking for. This makes the quest much easier.

In one house, we wandered about independently and bumped into each other in the foyer. Simultaneously we said, "I really like this house." It ranked high in most of the important categories on both of our checklists. We bought the house, and we still live there. It's not perfect, but it has many of the qualities we like and we can live with its shortcomings. We'll probably be here for another thirty years.

The next time you shop for anything significant, spend some time thinking about it first. Whether it's a car, a house, a bicycle, a college education—or even a clock radio—it's worth the investment to study your real needs, wants, and dislikes before you go to the store. You might decide that you don't need to buy anything at all. Sometimes that's the best choice.

Chapter 22

TRUST FACTS, NOT OPINIONS

Pearl #22: Take the time to learn the facts before you pass along scary or inflammatory e-mails, rumors, or opinions.

Through the wonders of modern technology, people can readily share their opinions with the entire world. Blogs, discussion groups, social networking sites, chat rooms, Twitter, talk radio, and countless other mechanisms let anyone with a keyboard or a telephone spout off on any topic. Now you can hear multiple individuals making equally fervent claims regarding contradictory "facts" and "truths." So what can you believe? Was Barack Obama born in the United States or not? Does hormone replacement therapy increase the risk of heart disease in post-menopausal women or not? Are illegal immigrants a net drain on the American economy or a net contributor? Have extraterrestrials really visited the Earth? Ask five people, and you'll get seven opinions.

Sometimes, though, there is just one answer to a question. We can guess the answer, we can debate it, we can vote on it (which is the most ridiculous approach—beliefs do not alter facts), we can reason through the issue to deduce a likely conclusion, or we can express our opinions. Whenever possible, though, it's better to discover the truth.

I learned this lesson in graduate school. One evening I was chatting with my thesis advisor and a fellow graduate student, who were both big coffee drinkers. (I can't stand the stuff). We began discussing how cream or a powdered creamer might change the acidity of coffee. Being chemists, we discussed the likely effect of the cream on the coffee's acidity and tried to rationalize the result. Then my advisor, Stan, offered a radical suggestion. "Let's measure it," he proposed.

Stan got a pH meter from the lab. He poured a fresh cup of black coffee and measured its acidity. Then he added some cream, stirred it well, and measured the acidity again to see if there was any effect. As I recall (after all, it was 35 years ago), the coffee with cream was less acidic than the black coffee. Mystery solved! That night I realized that it's better to find a definitive answer to a question rather than simply debate the point or try to think logically through the problem to reach a conclusion.

This isn't always possible. Sometimes you don't have an appropriate measuring device. Certain things can't be "measured" in a way that provides a definitive answer to a question. In many cases, though, you can go beyond opinion or gut reaction to find a fact, resolve a debate, or judge the truth of a statement.

Consider the myriad chain e-mails that circulate through the Internet. They warn you about the latest catastrophic computer virus that will steal your identity and destroy your computer. They express outrage about one side or the other of a polarizing political issue. They make extreme claims about some religious, cultural, or historical topic, such as the doom and destruction in 2012 allegedly predicted by the ancient Mayan calendar or the massive conspiracy supposedly behind the September 11 attacks. The e-mails urge us to forward this vital information to everyone we know, thereby propagating the author's viewpoint regardless of how valid it is.

Most such messages are false, even though many of them have circulated through the Internet for years. Propagating them spreads fear, distrust, and misinformation to no useful end. While I can't "measure" these claims myself, other people have spent considerable time and effort checking out these messages and debunking—or occasionally confirming—them.

An excellent online resource is Snopes.com. One of my relatives used to forward to me all the e-mail warnings about scary viruses that she received from her gullible friends until I convinced her to check their credibility on Snopes.com first. Nearly all of them were either fakes or old news. If you take the time to perform such simple checks, you quickly learn that there is much more fear mongering than useful cautionary advice in such communications. Similarly, instead of falling for the latest conspiracy theory, no matter how vigorously expressed, study the facts. Read authoritative scientific and historical evaluations to draw your conclusions instead of succumbing to the often groundless claims of misguided zealots.

Politicians and media pundits, particularly conservative extremists, are notorious for stretching the truth to the breaking point. Simply shouting a falsehood repeatedly at the top of your lungs does not make it true. Websites such as Factcheck.org and Politifact.com publish the facts behind such questionable claims. Some such sites rate the truthfulness of claims on a scale such as: true, mostly true, half true, barely true, false, and flaming lie. I trust that sort of assessment a lot more than the shouts of people who are foaming at the mouth with rage.

Recently a friend mentioned something scary he had read about the health care bill passed by Congress early in 2010. This claim was *not* true, as a search of the Internet revealed in just a minute or two. I've learned to be skeptical of almost everything I hear and read about politics, particularly the inflammatory claims and counterclaims on sensitive, complex issues. It's well worth the time to learn as much as you can about such important topics by studying assessments from impartial analysts who prefer to reveal the truth instead of fanning the flames of conflict.

Beware of conclusions based on inaccurate premises or assumptions, as well as those reached through faulty logic. Here's an example of the former. Someone once posed to me this scientific conundrum: "If a mirror reverses images left to right," he asked, "why doesn't it also reverse images top to bottom?"

I puzzled over this for some time before I realized that his initial assertion was incorrect. A mirror does *not* reverse images left to right! If you stand in front of a mirror and move your left hand, the hand on the left side of your mirror image will also move. You might perceive it as being a reversal because if that were an actual person facing you instead of your reflection, it would be the other person's right hand that was moving synchronously with your left hand. But that's not what's happening with the mirror. So in reality, there's nothing to explain, because the original assertion was false. When someone is trying to convince you about their wild conspiracy theory, their implausible scientific conclusions, or their prediction of impending catastrophe, be sure that both their facts and their logic are sound before you get too worked up about it.

Sometimes learning the facts leads to a conclusion that conflicts with your world view or with your gut. Which are you going to believe? There's an old saying—variously attributed to the Swedish Army, the Boy Scouts, and others—that when the map and the terrain do not agree, you should believe the terrain. If the data and my opinion conflict, I'm going to go with the data, wherever it takes me. This doesn't always make me happy, but I do have to deal with reality. In my first performance evaluation after I began my professional career more than thirty years ago at Kodak, my manager wrote, "Karl is rarely caught without an opinion, but he is non-dogmatic and is willing to change his view in the face of evidence." I think this is a sensible attitude to have.

If you've ever passed along a provocative chain letter or rumor without checking its credibility first, you might feel a bit silly if someone points out that the claim you're propagating is false. As the late U.S. senator Daniel Patrick Moynihan said, "Everyone is entitled to his own opinion, but not his own facts." Try to determine the facts before you spread an opinion.

Chapter 23

AN OUNCE OF PREPARATION

*Pearl #23: Even a little advance planning can help
you avoid disappointment, mistakes, and even disaster.*

*W*hen I began giving presentations at software conferences in the early 1990s, most speakers used plastic transparencies on an overhead projector for their visuals. Only a handful of speakers had begun using laptop computers with PowerPoint or other presentation software. I once taught a full-day tutorial at a local conference when I was living in Rochester, New York. I packed up my boxes of transparencies and headed to the conference site. In the middle of my talk, I noticed I was running out of transparencies. Suddenly I realized that I had brought only two of the four boxes of transparencies I needed for this full-day tutorial. Uh-oh. Kind of embarrassing.

Fortunately, the man who was running the conference saved my bacon. I had sent him an electronic version of my presentation in advance, which he had installed on his laptop. After lunch I was able to complete my presentation using his laptop in lieu of my missing transparencies.

That was a close call. I learned my lesson, though. From then on I have *always* used a checklist to prepare for my speaking and consulting engagements. I already had created a travel checklist, but since this was a local event with no travel involved, I didn't bother to think carefully about what I needed to bring with me. I never made that mistake again.

My travel checklist has evolved over the years. I use it both for business and vacation travel. Different sections of the checklist remind me what to take along depending on which class I'm teaching. A separate section lists items I might take with me when I am driving somewhere instead of flying, like my favorite pillow and my stuffed teddy bear.* I have a supplemental checklist for international travel that reminds me to bring my passport, visa, international driver's license, power plug adapters, camera, and so forth.

I am religious about using the checklist to plan my trip and pack my bags. It helps me take along the right amount and the right kind of clothing, all of my toiletries, the right frequent-flyer and car-rental cards, and the noise-canceling headphones that make long flights more bearable. It's also convenient to have a record of everything that is in my suitcase, should it be eaten by the airline's subterranean baggage-handling creatures. Thanks to these checklists, I have never reached a destination and found that I was missing a pair of socks or my laser pointer.

You might laugh at my little checklists, but I tell you, they work. When I described my travel checklist to a fellow software consultant, he chuckled, held up his index finger, and said, "My checklist has one thing on it: slides." But then he told me about the time he attended a conference to deliver a half-day tutorial presentation, only to discover that he was scheduled to teach—but had not brought along slides for—a full day. Sounds like my colleague needs a better checklist.

I'm comfortable with checklists and procedures because I'm a process kind of guy. Process people are not just worrywarts or sticklers for

---

* Just kidding about the teddy bear. Not kidding about the pillow.

following "the rules." We've simply discovered that taking a structured and systematic approach to complex, error-prone activities is easier and less stressful than winging it and keeping our fingers crossed.

For the same reason, I write down the particulars of significant agreements I make with others to avoid confusion, mistakes, and hard feelings. I've spent much of the last fifteen years traveling to corporations around the world to deliver training courses. I always use a simple speaking agreement for these events. This agreement contains:

- the particulars of the event (topic, location, number of attendees, dates and times, and contact person);

- my requirements for the facility, such as a projector for my laptop, flipcharts and markers, microphone, and instructions for setting up the room;

- information about the student handouts and textbooks we will use in the course;

- financial details, including my money-back guarantee; and

- contingencies for unexpected occurrences that could disrupt the planned event.

This all fits on one page, and it works just fine for most engagements. Occasionally a client will have a legal department that wants to get in on the action, so they create a vastly longer and more complex agreement that we have to negotiate.

I have another consultant friend who loathes paperwork. He never uses a written agreement with his clients if he can get away without one. Luckily, he hasn't encountered any problems with this approach— yet. But I've had some experiences when having a written speaking agreement was quite valuable.

Once I flew to Newark and drove to the New Jersey countryside to teach a three-day class at a large company. The next morning I went to the building where the class was to be held. No one was there to meet me. I finally was able to reach my contact person on the phone. She thought the class was going to begin the *next* day and run for three days. Ah, this explained why the receptionist didn't know what I was talking about.

I pulled out the speaking agreement. Sure enough, I was there on the correct date. By not reading the agreement carefully, my contact had miscommunicated to all the students in the class. We had only two days to cover everything we were originally going to cover in three. Now, if I had shown up a day late for a class I was supposed to teach, I'm sure there would have been financial consequences, not to mention the inconvenience to all of the students. In this case, we were able to work it out, but it was a mistake that didn't have to happen.

Besides checklists, I like binders. When my wife and I go on a trip, I often prepare a binder with a tab for each day of the trip. Behind each tab I keep copies of the confirmations for the hotels or bed and breakfasts where we plan to stay, a list of wineries and other attractions we plan to visit (there's not much point in traveling if wine isn't involved), maps and directions printed from the Internet, contact information for people we're going to see, pages copied from a tour book, and so forth. We always make reservations for accommodations in advance because I have too many childhood memories of my father getting more and more frustrated as he looked for a motel vacancy when we were on a family trip.

This sort of organization and planning doesn't detract a bit from our enjoyment of the trip. It's nice to know that all the information we need is organized in one convenient place. We also get to spend more time enjoying ourselves because we don't have to spend time on logistics. Who wants to waste even a few hours of their precious vacation looking for a place to sleep? It's been helpful to have the documentation along when there was some disagreement with the hotel about the room cost or the nights of our stay. We aren't constrained by our planned-out itinerary. We spend our days as we wish with the help of a general plan, and we adjust it as we go along. The plan just helps us get started.

The binder can help reduce the chaos and stress associated with a long journey. It doesn't prevent every risk, of course. When we moved from New York to Oregon in October of 2000, our binder did not help us avoid hitting the largest pothole in South Dakota, which dented and cracked a wheel rim and created a steady air leak in that tire. Nor did our planning anticipate the car wreck that required me to leave my car in Boise for ten weeks for repairs. But that's another story.

Human memories are fallible. Our brains must keep track of a huge amount of information, and important details just fall through the cracks sometimes. We misremember the details of a conversation with a contractor, or we forget to record a commitment in our Day-Timer or BlackBerry. Keeping simple records will ensure that all participants involved in a given activity agree on the details. It will help you avoid disappointment and disagreement. I'm not suggesting you write a contract the next time you want to meet your friends for lunch. There's no value in taking any process to a silly extreme. I use procedures and checklists to reduce the risk of a foul-up whenever the potential impact could be significant. Process is a structure, not a straitjacket. It's just a tool that helps things go more smoothly than they might otherwise.

Preparation can even save your life. My brother participates in many outdoor activities, often in desolate areas in the mountains and deserts of Idaho. Bruce is incredibly well prepared for any potential problem. He always goes exploring with a companion, never alone. He carries an emergency GPS tracking device, space blankets, water purifier, food for several days, flashlight, knife, rope, first aid kit, spare batteries for all electrical devices, and so forth. All of his experience as a leader of Boy Scouts—whose motto is "Be Prepared"—paid off one day in early 2010.

Bruce and a friend were exploring Hart Creek Canyon in the Idaho desert, many miles from civilization. He slipped on an ice-covered rock in a stream and fell, severely fracturing his thighbone. This is a very serious injury. It's easy for the razor-sharp edges of the broken bone to sever your femoral artery, in which case you might bleed to death.

All of Bruce's training and preparedness got him through this crisis. He kept his wits about him and didn't panic. He used much of the emergency gear he had with him, and it all worked. He stayed fairly warm and dry as his friend went for help. The emergency GPS tracking device—and its monitoring staff—did its job.

After lying there for three hours alone as daylight waned and the canyon grew colder, Bruce's friend returned with a rescue team. The rescuers winched Bruce out of the deep canyon on a litter and flew him to a hospital in Boise by helicopter, where he underwent several hours of surgery. His leg now contains a lot of metal, but he has recovered amazingly well.

Most of the time you won't need your emergency preparations. I hope you never do. But if you do, having the right items available and keeping a cool head just might keep you alive.

You might be able to think of times when you wish you had done a bit more planning or a bit more checking. Maybe you wound up on a camping trip without the air mattress. Perhaps the stew you cooked over the campfire would have been tastier with the salt that you left sitting on your kitchen counter. The dog's leash might also be a good thing to bring along next time. Every such oversight can lead to a checklist improvement that will make your future trips go just a bit smoother. That's the essence of process improvement.

You might not agree with my philosophy that an ounce of preparation can save you a ton of aggravation. Maybe you're a spontaneous type who thinks checklists are a waste of time. You could be right. Let's try an experiment. Let's take a trip together. I'll use a checklist to help me plan and pack, and you just do what you normally do. We'll see who runs out of underwear first.

Chapter 24

EVERYTHING IS NEGOTIABLE

*Pearl #24: You can almost always negotiate a
better deal if you focus on a win-win outcome.*

When you see the price tag on an item in a store, don't take
it too literally. Prices that appear to be cast in concrete often
have some flexibility. Almost everything is negotiable. Long ago a friend
taught me these magic words. She liked to frequent garage sales and
antique stores to flesh out her collection of Chinese cloisonné vases.
She told me that if you politely ask, "Can I do any better on the price?"
you will often spend less than the sticker price. That strategy works
surprisingly often.

In the United States, dickering on price is customary at antique
stores, yard sales, and flea markets. If you go to a video store and buy a
big-screen TV, audio system, and Blu-ray player, you should be able to
negotiate a hefty bundle discount. And no one should pay list price for
a car. Organizations like Consumer Reports make it easier to negotiate

by selling reports that list the dealer invoice cost of vehicles and options. This data lets you negotiate up from a cost position, rather than down from a list-price position. I applied this strategy the last time I bought a car, and it worked well.

I've discovered that you can negotiate prices in many other circumstances too. Look at it this way: if you don't ask, you'll certainly pay the full price, but if you inquire, you might save a few bucks. I bought a pair of shoes at a mall store last year. I smiled and asked, "Can I do any better on the price?" The salesman said they did have a coupon for twenty-five dollars off any purchase over one hundred and fifty dollars. He didn't spontaneously mention the coupon; I had to ask. So I paid a few dollars for some waterproofing wax for my new shoes, which pushed the total price above one hundred and fifty dollars, and I got the twenty-five dollars off. When I bought another pair of shoes at the same store a few months later, I asked if they had any coupon deals or other specials. No, they didn't, but the salesman told me to pick out any pair of socks I wanted for free.

Some medical offices will give you a discount if they don't have to hassle with insurance paperwork. Both my chiropractor and my optometrist reduce my bill because my medical insurance doesn't cover alternative medicine or eye care services.

I bought a nice jacket in a clothing store in San Francisco a couple of years ago. The store had a big sale going on. Although the jacket wasn't marked as being part of the sale, I asked the salesman if the sale price applied. He said, sure, he could do that. Then he told me that they were having another sale later that week, so he could give me an even better price on the jacket. I wound up paying less than half price, just by asking.

My yard needed some landscaping work one summer. One landscaping company, which I had used several times before, quoted me a price of eight hundred and fifty dollars. I asked if they could possibly do the job for eight hundred, please. They replied that since I was a repeat customer, yes, they could do it for eight hundred.

Not one hour before I wrote this chapter, I was in a sporting goods store looking for new running shoes. A knowledgeable young salesman helped me pick out a pair that seemed fine for my not-so-ordinary feet. Running shoes: $84.99. Support insoles: $19.99. Getting 20 percent off just by asking: priceless (actually, $21.00).

There are various negotiating tricks you can try. Instead of just asking for a discount, look for a reason that the merchant might be willing to give you a lower price. Maybe you've bought from them before, or you're willing to take a demo product instead of a brand-new one in the box. Perhaps you'd prefer to buy an item from them right there, right then instead of going home and ordering the product from an online source. Some stores will let you use a competitor's discount coupon. It never hurts to ask.

Sometimes you can save a bit on a major purchase by offering to pay for it in cash rather than with a credit card, because the merchant has to pay a fee of 2 or 3 percent on each credit card transaction. Debit card payments cost the merchant less than credit cards, so you might get a modest discount if you pay by debit card. Beware, though: if you pay by cash or debit card, you might not have certain consumer protections that your credit card provides.

Occasionally a customer who wishes to buy some software training products or services from my company, Process Impact, wants to negotiate. That's fine; I'm not offended. I'll work with the person to see if we can agree on a discount, typically on a volume purchase or a bundle of products and services. I also offer discounts for members of certain professional organizations. Once, though, a prospective client asked me to give her a hefty discount of several thousand dollars on a training class just because her budget was limited. Sorry, no can do.

You don't win every negotiation. I've sometimes used another landscaping company that charges a lot more than the company I mentioned above because usually they do a better job. But they've been completely inflexible on pricing, even at times when I know they're hurting for business. That's okay. I can use the other landscapers who do a good-enough job at a significantly lower cost. I'm willing to pay extra for quality, but only when it makes a real difference.

Whenever you're negotiating with someone, you need to do it respectfully and you need to work toward a win-win outcome. No one should feel as though he's being exploited. As Fisher, Ury, and Patton point out in their book *Getting to Yes*, it's important to keep the interests of all parties in mind instead of simply staking out a position and defending it to the death.* This premise applies whether you're negotiating a price at the store, negotiating commitments at work with your boss, or trying to work out a problem with a neighbor.

When I moved into my current house in 2000, I began hearing tinkling noises one evening. Upon investigation, I found that a nearby house boasted the world's largest collection of wind chimes. There were dozens of chimes positioned all around the outside of the house. The house was a couple of hundred feet away, but it was upwind from me, so the sound wafted right into my bedroom on the breeze. There's a large expanse of open space between our houses, so there was nothing to block the sound.

I hate wind chimes. I realize that many people find them pleasant and soothing, but I just find them irritating, particularly when I'm trying to sleep with the window open. That's the problem with wind chimes: unlike music, chimes are on twenty-four hours a day, seven days a week, and they have no volume control. I believe that it should be a capital offense if you own wind chimes that can be heard beyond your property line. You might think I'm exaggerating. You would be mistaken.

---

*   Roger Fisher, William Ury, and Bruce Patton, *Getting to Yes: Negotiating Agreement Without Giving In*, 2nd ed. (New York: Penguin Books, 1991).

So I went to meet my new neighbor and discuss the wind-chime situation. Since there were only certain chimes that really penetrated into my ears, I was hopeful that he would agree to remove or relocate those chimes. However, Captain Windchime wasn't very receptive to my overtures, even though I didn't tell him about my capital-offense philosophy. I tried to identify which chime was the most irritating and asked if he might be able to move that one to another side of his house. Captain Windchime grumbled, "It costs me money for the mounting racks whenever I have to move or install the chimes." Remembering my focus on a win-win solution, I offered to buy a new mounting rack for him. He seemed surprised by my suggestion, and he grumbled slightly less after that. He even moved the most irritating chime and didn't ask me to pay for the rack. It wasn't a perfect solution, but it was an improvement, and I appreciated his cooperation. Fortunately, Captain Windchime and his collection moved away a few years later. Problem solved.

It's been an eye-opener for me to realize how frequently you can save money in a transaction simply by asking. Since I first wrote this chapter, I've saved money through negotiation on a set of car tires, a maintenance contract for my home's heating systems, several magazine subscription renewals (ask if you can get the same rate offered to new subscribers), and renewing my cable TV, Internet, and phone service. It doesn't work every time, but it works more often than you might expect. And no one has ever refused to sell me a product or service simply because I asked if I could do any better on the price.

Chapter 25

IS IT QUALITY OR IS IT CRAP?

*Pearl #25: It usually takes just a little more
time, effort, attention, or money to do a
high-quality job instead of a mediocre one.*

Hold your hand up in front of your face, keeping about an inch between your thumb and index finger. Do you see that gap? Much of the time, that's the difference between quality and crap. That's all it takes. Think of that inch as being the "crap gap." To go from crap to quality, sometimes you just need to think, listen, or plan a little more, write a little more down, measure and test a little more, or ask one more question. To be fair, sometimes it takes more effort than that to change a lousy situation into a high-quality outcome, but often it does not.

Here's an example. A few years ago, I needed to get my home's heating system cleaned and checked to make sure it was ready for winter. A technician I'll call Fred came out to work on it. Fred exuded the cocky air of being God's gift to the heating and air-conditioning industry. (Memo to Fred: you aren't.) After he made a final adjustment at the furnace, I asked Fred if he should test the system to make sure everything was okay. "Not necessary," he replied. "You're in good shape."

A few weeks later we experienced a cold snap. Sure enough, the furnace did not work. In his last action, Fred had broken a wire, which would have been immediately obvious had he taken five minutes to test the system. Instead, we were chilly for a while and Fred's company had to send a technician back to our house—at their expense—to make the repair. Just recently, the company Fred worked for went bankrupt. Coincidence? You be the judge.

I'm continually astonished by the number of mistakes I see made by companies of all kinds. Being self-employed as an independent consultant and trainer, I've sent hundreds of invoices to clients for services or products. An amazing number of these invoices disappear somewhere in the company. I'm forced to follow up when payment doesn't come on time. Usually I discover that some kind of internal error resulted in the company's failure to process my invoice. Mistakes do happen, but if I paid my bills the way some of my clients pay theirs, I'd probably be in jail.

Whenever I encounter a problem like this, I wonder if it's a process problem, as opposed to a random human error. I often ask the person I'm dealing with what they can change to avoid similar errors in the future. Most people don't seem to think in terms of process, though. Their attitude is, "Well, somebody just made a mistake. There's nothing we can do about it." Sometimes that's true, but often these kinds of problems indicate a shortcoming in the way the company is approaching its business, such as continuity problems when a particular individual changes jobs or leaves the company. All companies should be committed to ongoing process improvement, seeking opportunities to make their business operations ever more efficient and effective. Problems provide an immediate indication that some process improvement, or perhaps employee training, is in order.

In 2001 I traveled to Australia and New Zealand to speak at some software conferences. They are both wonderful countries with delightful people, lovely scenery, great food, and fine wine. After I returned, I took two enlarged photographs from the trip to a local frame shop to get them matted and framed. With the help of the store manager, I selected frames and double mattes for the two photos. When I picked up the framed photos a week or two later, they didn't look right to me. It turned out the framer had taken the *inner* matte I had selected from one order and the *outer* matte from the other order and used that combination on both photos. That is, they were both done wrong. The result was that the store had to redo the mattes on both pictures, costing them time and money and delaying delivery to me.

I found this error puzzling because the orders were written down correctly. All the framer had to do was check the order to make sure she was doing it right. The woman who worked on my order did an excellent technical job of framing, but this was a silly mistake that didn't have to happen. It's that small crap gap again. It reminds me of an aphorism I first heard from my high school chemistry teacher: "When all else fails, read the directions." That frame store's not in business anymore either.

Shortly after we moved into our new home in Portland, we decided to get some vertical blinds installed in our bedroom. I took a drawing of the three windows and their dimensions to a local blinds specialty store. It took three tries for them to get the blinds installed right. First, the installer used mounting brackets that were too short and didn't test them before he raced out the door. We couldn't even open the blinds all the way. After he replaced those brackets on a subsequent visit, we discovered that the blinds were too narrow to cover the windows, so a second correction was necessary. Again, these preventable errors wasted money and time and led to aggravation. I've heard that "haste makes waste," and I've been advised to "measure twice, cut once." Why don't all professional craftspeople respect the truth in these old adages?

I've been guilty of quality mistakes myself. When I was working as a software developer long ago, I wrote a small program that moved completed files from the developer's own computer disk to the production disk where users could access the files. First the program copied the files from the developer's disk to the destination disk, and then it erased the original files from the developer's disk. Everyone in my group used this program, including me. It worked just fine, at least initially.

One day one of our developers came to me, justifiably upset. He had run this little program but didn't get the results he expected. Sure enough, it had erased the files from his own disk, but they did not appear on the destination disk where he was trying to send them. There was an omission in my program: it didn't check to make sure the files were copied successfully before deleting the original files. In this case, the copy operation had failed, probably because the destination disk was full.

As a result of my stupidity in not performing this check, my colleague lost an entire day of work. He was very angry with me, and I didn't blame him a bit. I'm surprised he didn't punch me in the nose. After that, I made sure that similar programs I wrote didn't make this same kind of bonehead error. It's called "defensive programming," and I should have known to practice it in the first place. If it's true that we learn from our mistakes, I must be a genius by now.

Many quality errors are simply nuisances. Sometimes, though, a sloppy mistake can be dangerous, such as mistakes made by medical professionals. I came close to just such a mistake a few years ago. I wasn't seeing as well as I would like using my computer-distance glasses, so I went to see my optometrist, who wrote me a new prescription. When I got the glasses, I just couldn't get used to them. My vision seemed just as bad as before.

Finally, I returned to the optometrist and found that he had made an error. He recorded my new optical correction in the medical chart properly, but he wrote the prescription for the *previous* correction. I had bought a new pair of lenses that were exactly the same as the previous pair. I got my money back, the optometrist wrote the correct prescription, I filled it at a different optical shop, and I changed optometrists. In this case no physical harm was done, but you can certainly imagine the damage that could result from an analogous error in medication or a surgical procedure. There's no excuse for that kind of sloppiness, especially when it comes to a person's health and well-being.

Sometimes you can defend against crap, sometimes you can't. I once had a friend who had a house built. Jim went to the construction site every day to make sure the house was being built properly. Jim made sure every aspect of construction looked right and that each item being installed was the right one, not a cheaper substitute. Jim ended up with a fine house, but at the end of the project, his contractor told him, "If everyone was as diligent as you are, I couldn't make money building houses." That's sad. The contractor was saying that he had to cut corners to make a profit. I'd rather pay a little more up front to get the quality I expect and to know that I would have fewer problems down the road.

My friend Rick also had a custom house built. He wasn't as rigorous as Jim about monitoring construction. When he moved in, he discovered that a closet at one end of the house was too shallow. He couldn't even put a coat hanger on the rod in that closet and close the door. The contractor had built the house one foot shorter than the blueprints specified!

How in the world did that happen? It probably began as a simple misreading of the plans. Maybe the men who dug the foundation read a 58 as a 57 or something like that. The error compounded as construction progressed. I wonder if anybody noticed that some of their boards were cut a foot too long or that they had flooring left over after finishing that end of the house. That tiny original mistake led to a major difference between the quality Rick expected and the house his contractor built. There was nothing he could do about it after the house was finished.

People make mistakes. That's a fact we have to accept. What is not acceptable to me, however, is making the same mistakes repeatedly and failing to learn from them. The process improvement mindset is really more of a process awareness. No one sets out to do a lousy job. I like to believe everyone goes to work each day to do the best job they can, based on what they know at that time. When things go awry, it's up to each of us to think about how to prevent a similar problem in the future, perhaps by modifying the processes we use, perhaps by using better quality methods to catch errors early. In many cases all it takes is more attention to detail, some ongoing improvement thinking, and a little more care to prevent quality from turning to crap.

Consider your own life. You can probably identify situations when it wouldn't have been much harder to do a high-quality job instead of letting it slide. Sometimes we rush to finish a task, cutting corners to get it done on time. I learned the folly of this short-sighted approach from a sign on the wall of a chemistry classroom: "If you don't have time to do it right, when will you have time to do it over?" We usually find the time to fix the problems that arise from low-quality work, and it almost always costs more effort, money, and goodwill than if we had just done it right the first time. Keep the crap gap in mind the next time you're tempted to take a shortcut.

Part 5

CAUTIONARY PEARLS

The world can be a scary place. Many things can go wrong; many things can harm you. I've had numerous small experiences that revealed some of these dangers to me, and I share some of those experiences in these chapters. Sometimes the danger arises from people we don't know, such as other drivers on the road. In other cases, the problem is closer to home, such as a relative who conveys poor advice or a parent who doesn't take advantage of a "teachable moment" to help a child grow into the best adult he can be.

Often through painful experience, I've learned how to avoid some of these risks or minimize the dangers. Each chapter in this section suggests ways that you, too, can be alert to these potential pitfalls and perhaps avoid them. These tips might make your life a bit easier and safer than it would be otherwise.

Chapter 26

CAN YOU SEE ME NOW?

Pearl #26: Whether you're riding a motorcycle, driving a car, or navigating through life, watch out for the blind spots that conceal potential risks to your well-being.

When I was thirty-two years old, I got some of the best advice anyone ever gave me. To make my life a little more adventurous, I had decided to learn to ride a motorcycle. I consulted my brother, who had many years of motorcycling experience, and bought one of the models Bruce suggested. Then he gave me that world-class advice: take a Motorcycle Safety Foundation riding course. I took the course within three months. It was one of the smartest things I ever did.

The instructors of the MSF course taught me the mechanics of riding a motorcycle. Even more important, they provided a wealth of safety guidance and riding tips. I still keep their recommendations in mind every time I ride. When I began riding, I picked up some bad habits from friends who were experienced motorcyclists. The MSF course corrected those and helped ingrain safe riding habits into my brain. One of the most important things I learned was to watch out for blind spots.

A fender bender on a motorcycle can result in a compound fracture or worse. Motorcycles are smaller than cars, so you have to make sure other drivers can see you. The MSF instructors shared statistics about the types of collisions that are most common among motorcyclists. Many accidents happen when a driver doesn't spot the bike and pulls out or turns left in front of it.

I try to be particularly aware of those dangerous situations. When I'm coming up to a vehicle sitting at a cross street, I check to see if the driver is looking right at me, and I watch to see if his wheels start moving as I approach him. When I approach parked cars next to my lane, I look for people sitting on the driver's side who might open a car door right in front of me. If I see a vehicle behind me when I'm approaching a stop, I'll tap my brake a couple of times, hoping the driver will spot the flashes and realize that I'm slowing down. You can't be too careful.

You have to be aware of the blind spots that other drivers have. I learned never to ride near the rear quadrant of another vehicle, particularly larger vehicles like SUVs, minivans, and trucks, because the drivers might not see me there. Now I always stay far enough behind a vehicle so that, if it were to swerve into my lane, I would not be at risk.

In the course, I also learned how important it is to be aware of my own blind spots. The MSF instructors taught us not only to check our mirrors when we want to change lanes but also to look over our shoulders to make sure we haven't missed anything. This is a good habit when driving a car as well. Being aware of blind spots, other vehicles, pedestrians, and similar potential dangers is called situational awareness.

Just as when we're on the road, we have blind spots in the rest of our lives. We might not see our own negative behaviors. For instance, I like to be quick and witty, so I frequently make remarks that are intended to amuse and generally do. Sometimes, though, I inadvertently cross the line and offend someone. I never intend to cross that line, but people have different tolerances for joking around. I always feel bad when I've offended someone with a comment that was more barbed than I intended. I try to pause and think before making a wisecrack, but that is contrary to my nature. I haven't been as successful at building in those pauses as I'd like, although I'm getting better.

Sometimes we are blind to our own medical issues, both mental and physical. I recently read a biography of a famous engineer. Although his mother had died of colon cancer and he had already lost a kidney to cancer himself, he ignored the rectal bleeding that he periodically experienced. By the time he finally had it checked out, his doctor discovered advanced colon cancer. The doctor had wanted to remove polyps from his colon years earlier, but the engineer had put it off. Within months after having much of his colon removed, he died at the age of sixty-five.

Society is more aware of this serious—and common—disease today. As my own doctor says, no one needs to die from colon cancer, because it can easily be detected, and even prevented, through a colonoscopy. I can understand why someone would want to avoid a colonoscopy. I was nervous when I had my first one at age fifty. Everyone agrees that the preparation is no fun, but there was nothing to the procedure itself, thanks to the sedation used. The whole experience just wasn't that horrible, and it was good to get a clean report. I'm glad I did it.

Men traditionally shy away from doctors even when they don't feel well. No one wants to get scary medical news. However, if there's a serious problem, you're better off knowing about it earlier rather than later. The blind spot that blocks your view of medical problems literally can be deadly.

Other types of behavioral blind spots can be difficult to detect. I have a close friend, one of the nicest and smartest people I've ever known, who suffered a brain injury in an automobile accident twelve years ago, thanks to an idiot on a cell phone who rear-ended his stopped car. (Please don't talk on your cell phone or send text messages while driving; your brain could be the next one to go.) Norm suffers both physical and cognitive impairments from the brain injury. This led to some blind spots in his behavior (but fortunately not literal blind spots in his vision, although he does experience double vision in both eyes). Norm now lacks the controls most of us have that keep us from talking at excessive length or in excessive detail. If you ask him a question, sometimes he'll go on and on enthusiastically until you stop him.

Norm is aware that he's subject to these sorts of behavioral blind spots, but he can't detect when he's caught in one. Therefore, he arranged a system of hand signals with his partner. Anytime she sees this excessive talking behavior, such as at a dinner party, she'll show him the "Norm, shut up" hand signal. You might need a little help from your friends to deal with your own blind spots.

Sometimes we're blind to the behaviors of others who are close to us. Parents sometimes don't see—or don't accept—trouble signs in their children. A woman I know had to rush her nineteen-year-old daughter to the emergency room because she was vomiting uncontrollably. It turns out the girl was terribly dehydrated and somewhat malnourished. She had been eating almost nothing because her fiancé had asked her to lose weight. Her mother, while very engaged in her daughter's life, had had no idea that her daughter had an eating disorder. It took five bags of intravenous fluid to rehydrate her.

We also can have blind spots in our relationships with other people. Do you have friends who don't return your calls anymore? Has your spouse or partner become more distant or less affectionate? Do colleagues sit at a different table at lunch instead of joining you as they used to? These could all be signs of a problem that is not out on the table yet. The problem could be you.

I once had a coworker—I'll call him Jeremy—who did not get along well with any of the managers he had over the years. As he moved from position to position within the corporation, there was always some reason Jeremy would give about why his current manager was a moron who didn't appreciate his talents and hard work. The sole common factor in all of these situations was Jeremy. Sure, we'll all have bosses and colleagues that we don't get along with for one reason or another. But when you clash with *all* of your managers or with *all* of your coworkers, perhaps it's time to look in the mirror.

Companies and other organizations can have blind spots too. They might not detect looming competitors, shifts in market demands, or technology trends that could put them out of business. Just ask the manufacturers of buggy whips, typewriters, slide rules, and instant cameras. It's a good idea to scan the horizon continually for sea changes that might make for rough sailing in the future. Baseball player Satchel Paige once advised, "Don't look back. Something might be gaining on you." In my view, if something really is back there, I want to know about it. I need to know about it.

Think about your own blind spots. What issues and concerns do you sweep under the rug in the hope that they'll just go away? Relationships do not heal themselves. Businesses do not fix themselves. Serious diseases rarely cure themselves. Sometimes I'm not crazy about reality, but it's all I've got, so I have to deal with it. My wife and I have long held this philosophy: it's better to deal with a concern before it becomes a crisis. This can lead to some uncomfortable conversations, but it's better than coming home one day to find the closet empty, the suitcases gone, and a note on the table.

Chapter 27

DODGING BULLETS

Pearl #27: A close call that scares you but doesn't do any real harm can lead to positive change—and might even save your life.

"**W**hew, that was a close one!" You've doubtless breathed this sigh of relief after the accident that almost-but-didn't-quite happen. You take a deep breath, wait for your pounding heart to calm down, and drive on your way, relieved that no metal was bent or bones broken. Such a near tragedy provides an excellent learning opportunity if you think about why the accident almost happened and how you could avoid a similar situation in the future.

It's true that we learn from our errors. Even better is to learn from a minor mistake that could have had much worse consequences. Let me tell you about some dodged-a-bullet experiences.

In 1986 I began riding a motorcycle. The mechanics of riding a bike aren't particularly challenging, although there's definitely some coordination needed among your right hand (throttle and front brake), left hand (clutch), left foot (gearshift), and right foot (rear brake). Once you've got those operations down, you can hit the road, right? Well, not really. There's a lot more to learn about handling a bike properly and riding safely.

Soon after I began riding, I was out for a cruise in the countryside in upstate New York. I came around a fairly sharp curve along the base of a steep hill that completely blocked my view to the right. The motorcycle drifted into the left lane. Either I was going a little faster than I should have or I just didn't lean the bike enough to the right, probably both. Had there been a vehicle in that oncoming lane coming around the blind curve, I would have been dead, no question about it. It was just good, dumb luck that kept me alive at that instant.

On the plus side, this experience scared the dickens out of me. The message that flashed through my mind was, "Whoa, you can really get hurt doing this if you do it wrong!" I wasn't riding like a madman, but obviously I wasn't adequately skilled in handling the motorcycle. In the past twenty-five years, I have always stayed aware of the hazards of motorcycle riding. Since that frightening day, I have not drifted into an oncoming lane or onto the shoulder, dumped the bike onto the ground, or had any other mishap. This was one of those near misses that got my attention and taught me a valuable lesson.

Some years ago, my wife went out to run some errands. She phoned me minutes later to report that she'd been in a car accident just a mile from the house. The accident was minor, and no one was hurt. I drove over anyway. A boy of about seventeen in a small pickup truck had rear-ended Chris's car on a major street. He just wasn't paying attention. The damage to both vehicles was trivial, merely some scrapes on the bumpers. The boy's mother offered to pay for the repairs to avoid involving the insurance companies, which was fine with us.

The boy was planning to go to his high school prom that night. He was pretty shaken up, as he should have been. I said to him, "Take this seriously, but don't let it ruin your prom." I actually think it's a good thing if young people can have a small accident like this shortly after they start driving. That way, they can grasp how easy it is to have a big accident and just how much damage a motor vehicle can do. A similar minor wreck just weeks after I first obtained my driver's license made me a much more careful driver. Because we never repaired the resulting dent in my father's old Opel, I was reminded of the experience every time I saw the car.

A lot of these dodged-a-bullet lessons deal with motor vehicles, because driving has the potential to become so dangerous so quickly. Once I was getting ready to make a right turn at an intersection. I saw a break in traffic and started to turn. Suddenly my passenger warned me about a pedestrian right in front of my car. If I had been alone in the car, I'm certain I would have hit that pedestrian. I simply did not check the crosswalk in front of the car before I started to move. Twenty-eight years later, I still remember the churning in my stomach at that way-too-close call, and I still diligently check for pedestrians, particularly when turning.

Near-misses can also motivate you to improve your safety practices around the house and workplace. I used to be an organic chemist. There's a lot of nasty stuff in the chemistry lab. Prudent lab workers use a variety of protective gear, such as goggles, face shields, rubber gloves, and aprons. I always wore a clear plastic, full-face shield when handling particularly corrosive materials. Before long, the shield was covered with pits from splattered acids that would have scarred my unprotected face. If that doesn't motivate a lab worker to take simple precautions, I don't know what will. I've had the same experience when using a string trimmer to edge my lawn. One time a tiny, but painful, speck of dirt landed in my eye. Ever since then I've worn goggles while using the trimmer. They are always speckled with dirt by the time I'm done. It's not an accident if you're prepared for it.

Sometimes people don't have the opportunity to learn from a small mistake before tragedy strikes. There was a horrible automobile accident in upstate New York in 2007. Two vehicles full of teenage girls were driving to a lakeside excursion, one week after they had all graduated from the high school in the same town where I used to live. The cell phone belonging to the driver of the lead vehicle was being used to exchange text messages with someone in the second car, although it's not certain who was using the phone. That driver smashed head-on into a tractor-trailer rig. All five girls in the lead vehicle were killed in the fiery crash.

Wouldn't it have been better if this inexperienced driver had run into something small like a mailbox, just enough of an accident to scare her and get her attention? Or, even better, if she had heeded the warnings of more experienced drivers about the dangers of distracted driving? These five girls never got the chance to learn a critical lesson.

Can you think of situations where you changed your safety behaviors because of the accident that didn't quite happen? It doesn't have to be something with a car. A relative of mine found a lump in her breast one day. A biopsy revealed that it was a benign tumor. She now has annual mammograms to find any future lumps as early as possible. Perhaps your neighbor's house was burglarized, finally motivating you to install those deadbolt locks.* Maybe you lost your purse, but instead of stealing your identity, some Good Samaritan returned your purse to you, cash and cards intact. This would be a good time to make copies of all of the cards you carry in your wallet in case it ever happens again. You might also remove from your wallet anything you don't really need to carry, like your Social Security card.

The next time you experience a close call, don't just breathe a sigh of relief. Look for ways to change your behavior to be more alert for similar problem situations in the future. Heading a problem off at the pass is a lot better than taking a trip to the emergency room.

---

* One night my neighbor's house in Rochester *was* burglarized. There were footsteps in the snow leading to my back door, then over to his back door. All of my doors had deadbolt locks; his did not. His house was burglarized; mine was not. Deadbolts are a cheap investment in security.

Chapter 28

KEEP GETTING UP

*Pearl #28: Parents need to look for "teachable moments"
to instill lifelong values in their children.*

"*I*f life gives you lemons, turn them into lemonade." "If at first
you don't succeed, try, try again." Such aphorisms allude to
the commendable personal characteristics of positive thinking and
perseverance. Sadly, these have never been my strong suits. I've always
been more of a glass-half-empty kind of guy. It's not that I go looking
for the black cloud around every silver lining. It's more that I spot the
downside of situations and wonder why things can't be better. I've also
never been long on tenacity and patience. I get frustrated easily when
things don't go well. It's easier to give up and move on to something else
than to keep pushing through the challenging situation.

Our personalities are partially shaped by the role models around us.
Typically, our first role models are our parents. My father was always
highly impatient and not a positive-thinking kind of person. He had

many capabilities, but he also became easily frustrated and irritated with people and situations that didn't shape up to his liking. We emulate and learn from those who are closest to us, for better or for worse. Dad asked me once where I got my sarcastic mouth. All he had to do was look in the mirror for an answer. Although I've long recognized these shortcomings in my personality, they're pretty well ingrained by now.

As I reflect on my youth, I can remember several situations in which my father missed an opportunity to help cultivate an attitude of patience and perseverance in me. Such situations are called "teachable moments." Ideally, a parent or mentor will spot such opportunities and use them to impart an "Aha!" insight to the young person.

Here's an example. My father loved football, so naturally I developed an interest in the game. When I registered for ninth grade a year after we moved to Boise, I saw a table where students could sign up to play football. I had never played on youth or school football teams, and I wasn't athletic in the least. I asked the coach how much you had to weigh to play on the lightweight team. "Fifty pounds," he replied, presumably tongue in cheek. I was a couple of years younger than most of the other students, so I was only twelve, but I was five-feet eight-inches tall. However, I weighed just 105 pounds—skinny and uncoordinated, a typical early adolescent boy. On the spur of the moment, I signed up for the East Junior High School ninth-grade lightweight football team, trying out for the position of offensive end. Ends normally wear jersey numbers in the 80s. The coach assigned me the number 63; perhaps that was an omen.

I imagine my father was both surprised and pleased that I went out for football. My parents bought me the necessary gear, including cleats, a mouth guard, and a face mask for the helmet because I had to wear glasses. I began attending practices after school, not having any idea what I was in for. Having never played organized sports and not being in any kind of physical condition, I got very sore. I also lacked any talent or ability, but I gave it a shot for a couple of weeks. I participated in one game but never got off the bench. After a few more days of practice, I concluded that it was a hopeless exercise and decided to quit the team. It was another week or so before I told my parents.

I'm sure my father was disappointed in me, but he didn't say anything. Looking back now, I wish we had sat down and discussed my reasons for quitting the football team and the implications thereof. This could have been an opportunity for him to instill a stronger sense of tenacity in me. He could have explained the importance of sticking with something either until I succeeded or until it became clear that I just couldn't do it and I wasn't enjoying myself. Instead, I just felt guilty about quitting and about the money my parents had spent on equipment. I've always believed that my father thought less of me for quitting the team. This was a missed teachable moment, although I didn't realize that at the time.

Here's another example. My father repeatedly said that he wanted both of his sons to reach the rank of First Class in the Boy Scouts. This is the third rank from the bottom, after Tenderfoot and Second Class. There are three additional ranks that culminate in the loftiness of Eagle Scout. I was an outstanding Cub Scout, and I really enjoyed those experiences. (Thanks for being such a good den mother, Mom.) Moving into Boy Scouts was the logical next step.

I might have been the worst Boy Scout in the history of the organization. I tried, but I was inept. I just couldn't seem to pick up the necessary Boy Scout skills easily, and I didn't feel like I fit in with the other boys in the troop. Being a typically uncoordinated adolescent didn't help. I went on just one Boy Scout camping expedition. Somehow, I managed to fall into a stream before we even reached the campsite. I just tripped over my own outsized feet. Eventually I achieved the rank of Second Class, earning the pitiful total of just a single merit badge, in bugling, of all things. I wasn't having much fun, and it didn't seem that

I was going to succeed, so eventually I dropped out of the Boy Scouts. Again, my father was disappointed.

As I got older, it occurred to me that my father didn't have the opportunity as a youth to do many of the things he wanted to do, such as participate in team sports and scouting. Perhaps he was attempting to relive his youth vicariously through his sons. When I dropped the ball (literally with football, figuratively with Boy Scouts), it really seemed to let him down. But I don't remember him ever asking me why I quit Boy Scouts and exploring whether there was some action we could take together that could help me succeed and achieve the goal—albeit *his* goal—of reaching First Class. Maybe tenacity would have become a stronger aspect of my personality if we had had some of these discussions about goals, commitments, and obstacles. And maybe, through these discussions, we would have learned to understand each other better.

Perhaps another role model could have made a difference for me. Uncle Carlin, my mother's younger brother, owned a dairy farm in Iowa with my grandparents. We didn't see Uncle Carlin, his wife, and my five cousins very often, but it was always a great treat when we did. Sometimes we would visit them at their farm. Only rarely would they visit us in Idaho, because it's so difficult for farmers to take a vacation. Uncle Carlin was just the coolest guy in the world to me. Farmers work extremely hard for modest compensation; I have great respect for what they do. Carlin never complained about the challenges and hardships of life as a farmer, though. He was always good-humored, funny, and upbeat.

Carlin fell on hard times in later years. He went through a nasty divorce that cost him a lot of money. Back pain forced him to give up the farming business, so he became a truck driver. Later he opened a small pizza restaurant that became a teen hangout in a small town in northern Iowa. Ultimately, he became the town's mayor. One day Pizza Hut moved to town. The Pepsi supplier informed Carlin that he could no longer sell to him because Pizza Hut and Pepsi were part of the same corporate empire. I thought this was a poor way to do business. So did Carlin, but he switched to Coke and kept on rolling.

Not surprisingly, the competition began sucking away his business. Carlin needed another source of income, so he opened a carpet-cleaning business. That worked well for him, but it was a physically demanding job, and he was getting older. One day he suffered a fall while cleaning a carpet and badly tore up his knee, an injury from which he never fully recovered.

As I observed Carlin's tribulations over the years, I admired his resilience. No matter what kind of ugliness life threw at him, he picked himself up, dusted himself off, looked around, and said, "Okay, what should I do now?" Whenever I spoke to him or saw him during those later years, he was the same old Carlin, smiling, good-natured, and tough as hell. When he injured his knee, I sent him a few hundred dollars to try to help out. He just mailed the check back to me with his thanks.

Talking to my mother about Carlin years later, she told me that, during some of those difficult times, he really *didn't* know what to do next, but I never got that impression from him. He reminded me of one of those big inflatable clown dolls that you can punch and knock over but that keeps popping back up again. That was Carlin. He just kept getting up.

I wish I'd had a chance to observe and try to emulate Carlin's perseverance and good humor at an earlier age. Perhaps this would have helped make it easier for me to think of lemonade, not lemons, to push through a barrier instead of bouncing off. I only saw Carlin every few years because we never lived nearby, but I always felt close to him.

One day Carlin went to the hospital to have surgery on a blocked carotid artery. He died on the gurney before they even got him onto the operating table. I cried when I heard the news. This time my Uncle Carlin didn't get up.

BE CAREFUL WHOSE ADVICE YOU TAKE

Pearl #29: Adults don't have all the right answers,
and sometimes they don't give good advice.

I bought my first electric guitar when I was twelve. I've played ever since, although I'm still clearly an amateur. After learning a few chords, the next logical step was to form a band. I met a few kids at junior high school who were also musicians, and we started getting together once in a while. In ninth grade we formed an actual band named the Inmates, so-called because we often practiced at a home near the old Idaho State Penitentiary (plus, in 1966, we were trying very hard to be "in"). The band was a lot of fun, but anyone who has ever been in a musical group knows that conflicts can arise and that band members will come and go.

One member of the group, Art, also acted as our manager. He was beginning to line up some gigs for us around town. I wouldn't say we were going places yet, but we could see the path. One day a dispute arose between Art and me; I don't even remember what it was about. I think we were having a power struggle about who was going to exert the most influence over the band's direction. We were both pretty angry.

I shared my frustration with a beloved aunt who was visiting my family at the time. Not only was Aunt Riesie just supercool, she was in show business! She split her time between Los Angeles and New York City, where she worked as a stage actress and musician. She was even in the national touring companies of some major Broadway productions. So who would know more about this kind of problem than her? I explained the situation to Aunt Riesie. Her advice was simple: quit the band.

This seemed kind of drastic to me. I was having a good time in the Inmates, even if there were some clashes. But I trusted my aunt's judgment, so I tendered my resignation to the rest of the group. I regretted it for years. Since I had helped start the group, my quitting came as something of a shock to my bandmates. I don't think they saw my conflict with Art as a big deal, certainly not as severe as it seemed to me. My departure came at an awkward time, as we had a gig coming up. I felt bad about leaving the group in the lurch, but it was too late by then. Another guitarist soon took my place, and the band played on.

Not surprisingly, my quitting the band so abruptly led to some hard feelings. My family experienced a spate of mildly harassing phone calls, and my younger brother got hassled as well. Bruce wasn't someone you wanted to mess with, though. When a friend of one of the other band members leaped out in front of Bruce when he was riding his bicycle, Bruce just ran over the kid and kept on going.

From this experience, I learned that grown-ups don't always have the right answers. I took my aunt's advice because I trusted her experience with show business. Instead of advising me to quit, I wish she had counseled me to work out the differences with my bandmates. Kids don't always know how to work out their differences, though, so parents and other adults should help. Getting some ideas about how to solve problems, negotiate, and compromise would have been more helpful to me than just walking away. Instead, I left a good thing just as it was gaining momentum. Several of the band members went on to become professional caliber musicians, so perhaps I could have had many more years of fun with them had we made it past that friction point.

There's a happy ending to this story, though. A few months ago I learned that my fortieth high school reunion was coming up. I had never attended a reunion before and wasn't planning to go to this one. But then I received an e-mail from Art. He said the Inmates were going to reunite and play some songs at the reunion. They had played at a couple of earlier reunions, and their performances had gone over well. Art actually apologized for the shenanigans of our high school days, which I appreciated, and I told him how sorry I was that I had quit the band when I did.

So in July of 2010, my wife and I drove to Boise, and I was onstage with a guitar in my hands for the first time since 1969. It was a blast! We played our scheduled eight songs, then got called back to play three more by popular demand. It was a real treat to see my old friends Art, Bud, and Glen after all those years and to perform with them and some other excellent musicians, Jim, Greg, and Andy. Our personalities clicked well, we sounded pretty damn good, and everybody had a grand time.

While we were known in junior high school as the Inmates, I thought a good name for our reunion band would have been the Repeat Offenders. It was all I could have hoped for.

Chapter 30

DRIVING AS A
METAPHOR FOR LIFE

*Pearl #30: Some techniques that keep you safe
behind the wheel can also help protect you
from doomed relationships and other hazards of life.*

I suspect that one of the most nerve-racking things a parent can
do is teach a child to drive. My father taught me to drive in
our 1960 Opel station wagon on a deserted road in Idaho when I was
fourteen. In Idaho back then, you could get a driver's license at age
fourteen with driver's training and at age sixteen without. I picked up
the mechanics of operating a stick shift without much difficulty and
without burning out the clutch.

As we all know, operating the vehicle is but a small fragment of
knowing how to drive. It's more difficult to master the driving skills that
will ultimately keep you alive, such as how to negotiate traffic, follow
the rules of the road, and anticipate problems so you can dodge them

in time. These techniques are mastered only with years of experience, sometimes gained at the price of dented steel. I was fortunate that my father shared some excellent safety tips with me. I later found that these tips apply to many aspects of life besides driving.

You've probably heard someone describe a "deer in the headlights" look. A deer is crossing the road at night and is illuminated by an oncoming car's headlights. It freezes in place and stares at the lights. This usually does not lead to a happy outcome. My father taught me never to look right at an oncoming car with its high beams on. Instead, look at the white line on the side of the road just above your right front fender. This way you have enough peripheral vision to be aware of what's in front of you, but you're not going to lose your night vision entirely.

Sometimes you might see that you're headed for a crash in some aspect of your life, but you freeze up. Like the deer, you can't think of how to get out of the way before it's too late. Maybe the company you work for is headed for layoffs or possibly even going out of business. You put off looking for another job or developing new skills, telling yourself that they'd never let you go. But it can happen to anyone. My wife's two closest friends were laid off from Kodak, one with thirty years and one with thirty-two years of service.

Or perhaps you're in a relationship that you know is doomed, but you just can't find a way to escape and so you do nothing. You don't break off the engagement, or you stay married, suffering in silence for the sake of the children. If you're in a physically abusive relationship, you might even fear for your safety, yet you feel helpless with no resources and nowhere to go. It's really hard, but the earlier you can evade these types of obstacles, the better off you're going to be.

I have a friend who has been divorced twice. In each case, he thought marriage was a good idea at the time he got engaged, but as each wedding date approached, it became clearer to him that it was not a good idea. In both cases, he couldn't find the courage to break off the engagement. He went through with each wedding, and each marriage lasted just a few years before ending in divorce. Yes, it's embarrassing to admit that you don't want to proceed with a planned marriage, that you made a mistake. It's going to cause hurt feelings and cost some money if the wedding is imminent. Still, those consequences are much smaller than the price of actually getting married, regretting it, and ultimately splitting up after some period of unhappiness.

Try to find the courage. If the relationship is doomed, get out. If your relationship suffers from domestic violence, there are places to go for help in most cities. Don't be paralyzed by your fears or doubts, because the consequences of staying are just too severe.

Another lesson I learned from my father was to keep my eyes moving while I drive. It's easy to fixate on a particular point, maybe staring at the vehicle directly in front of you or at the intersection where you intend to make a turn. But this fixation can prevent you from seeing what else is happening around you. When driving, you need to continually scan for possible threats so you can react in time. When you see a car on a cross street pull up to an intersection, is the driver going to stop at the stop sign? If she does stop, will she see you coming and yield, or will she pull out right in front of you?

Very recently, I pulled into an apartment complex on my Meals on Wheels route. I saw a little girl, perhaps four years old, running diagonally across the parking lot. Sure enough, she was chasing an errant ball about fifty feet away. Where there is one child, there are often others, so I looked around until I spotted her playmates.

You can't count on other people, particularly children, to keep *their* eyes moving all the time and to see you coming. Scan the horizon, sweep your eyes from just in front of the car to farther out and back again, and keep looking for threats. Don't forget to look behind you too. Use your mirrors, but also watch out for the blind spots. What happened to that minivan you spotted in your rearview mirror a moment ago?

Did the driver turn when you weren't looking, or is he hovering off your quarter panel, just out of view? My father taught me well, handing down safety lessons that were reinforced when I took the Motorcycle Safety Foundation's riding class I described earlier.

This kind of situational awareness and anticipation is also a good idea in your daily life. Try to look over the horizon for long-term issues that you might have to deal with. Don't be caught by surprise because you didn't plan and anticipate. When I was in graduate school, the research and teaching assistants got paid their annual salary over eleven months; we weren't paid in August. I knew one couple, both fellow grad students, who never had any money in August because they didn't take the simple action of saving one-eleventh of their salary in all the other months. This doesn't seem complicated.

With experience and maturity, you get better at looking ahead and knowing how to react, both on the road and in your life. Just weeks after I received my first driver's license, I was involved in an accident. I was driving down the road, minding my own business, when an old man at a stop sign on my left slowly pulled out in front of me. I thought, "He's going to hit me," and by George, he did.

The damage was minimal, just a dent in the side of the car, but I was pretty shaken up. Do you remember those images in old comic books of a bundle of money flying away on wings? A similar image flashed through my mind: my driver's license with little wings on it, flying into the sunset. The other driver was seventy-one years old and drunk. I was fifteen and inexperienced. It's an accident that wouldn't happen to me today because I would see it coming. I would take actions to avoid it instead of just letting the other driver plow into me. I'm a much better defensive driver now, far more aware of what's going on around me.

What's happening around you that maybe hasn't entirely registered? Are you ignoring signals from your child that could indicate serious problems such as substance abuse, eating disorders, or criminal activities?

Are you turning a blind eye to the signs of abuse or victimization in a friend's life—or in your own? Are you not saving enough money for retirement, hoping to get by on Social Security and the kindness of strangers? Are you neglecting problems in your relationship because you don't want to face how serious they might be? Have you put off writing a will or buying life insurance because you don't like to think about death, thereby putting your family at risk of not having enough money should the worst happen?

Maybe it's because I'm the oldest child in my family, but I've always been a bit of a worrier. My mother tells me that when I was small and we were on a driving trip, I assigned myself the job of watching out for big trucks. I must have been good at the job, as no truck ever hit us. I do try to be aware of what's happening with myself and with the people I care about in my life. I try to plan enough for life's eventualities so that, when they happen, they aren't massively disruptive to the people who are affected.

For example, I have prepared a large binder labeled "Karl and Chris Have Left the Building." It contains pretty much everything a survivor would need to know about our family at the time one of us passes away: account numbers, passwords, insurance policies, contact information for the lawyer and the accountant, investments, information about my company, even funeral instructions and CDs of songs to play. My father had prepared a similar binder. When he died, the information in it helped my family deal with important practical matters at a stressful and confusing time. I didn't prepare the binder because I have a morbid fascination with death. I just realize and accept the fact that things happen. Given a choice, I'd rather see things coming and be ready to handle them.

Part 6

PROFESSIONAL PEARLS

I have a technical background both by education and by occupation. My education is in chemistry, although I only worked as a research scientist for a few years before moving into the software development field. I have experience as a photographic research scientist, computer programmer, business analyst, software manager, software quality engineer, process improvement leader, independent consultant, trainer, and author. Throughout these career activities, I've been fortunate to cross paths with a lot of smart people. Some of these people have provided me with powerful insights that still stick with me today.

In this section, I'll present some of the lessons I learned in various environments, ranging from the chemistry research lab to high school band. You don't need to know anything about chemistry, computers, or music to understand these lessons. That's one of the great things about these insights: although I learned most of them in professional contexts, they are broadly applicable to almost any type of work, and even to daily life. So read on and look for ways to apply to your own world these fragments of wisdom that I've been fortunate to acquire.

Chapter 31

THE CUSTOMER IS
NOT ALWAYS RIGHT

Pearl #31: It's dangerous to act on the assumption that the customer is always right, because sometimes customers are unreasonable, uninformed, mistaken, or in a bad mood.

Perhaps you've patronized a business that had a sign on the wall saying something like: "We have only two rules. Rule #1: The customer is always right. Rule #2: If the customer is wrong, see Rule #1."

It's fashionable to say that the customer is always right, and I've seen people do some pretty silly things because of this attitude. But in reality, the customer is *not* always right, and we all know it. Sometimes the customer is irrational, belligerent, or flat out wrong. We are all customers, and most of us are also suppliers of products or services, so we have experience on both sides of this issue. I prefer to say, "The customer is not always right. But the customer always has a point, and that point should be understood and respected." As a customer, you may not always get what you want when you have a need or a problem. But you're certainly entitled to have the service provider or the merchant take your concerns seriously and try to understand them so you can achieve a mutually satisfying outcome.

In some cases, it's downright dangerous to assume the customer is always right. When you go to see your doctor because you don't feel well, you are a customer and the doctor is a service provider. These days, there's a good chance you've researched your symptoms on the Internet and scared yourself half to death. Yes, your headache *could* be a malignant brain tumor the size of a grapefruit, but it's far more likely to have a more benign cause. Suppose a patient comes in to the doctor's office and says, "I have a brain tumor. Please remove it as soon as possible." No doctor is going to take a patient's self-diagnosis as fact and say, "Sure, no problem. Does tomorrow morning work for you?" The customer has a point: he has a headache. The doctor must respect that point, then use it as a starting point to determine the real underlying problem and what to do about it.

Okay, that was a silly example, but it's not far off. Some years ago I woke up with laryngitis. I couldn't speak a word. I made an appointment to see my doctor, but instead I had to see a substitute physician whom I had never met. Since I could not speak, I wrote my symptoms and questions on an index card. I handed the card to the physician when he walked into the examination room. He glanced at it for not more than one second then asked, "So, what's the problem today?" Well, I couldn't speak! That's why I'd taken the trouble to write up my side of the dialogue that I would normally have during a doctor's visit and tried to present it to him. I wasn't happy that he completely blew me off. He did not respect the premise that the customer always has a point. I never went to that doctor again.

Software development is one area in which I've seen people abuse the notion that the customer is always right. A software project often begins with a customer presenting his needs to a business analyst. The analyst explores the customer's problem and writes a requirements specification that communicates those needs to other technical people, who then develop an appropriate solution.

It is common for customers involved in this kind of discussion to describe not their actual requirements but rather proposed solutions. A skilled business analyst can detect when the "need" that's been presented is really a solution idea and will ask questions to get at the underlying problem. Sometimes the customers don't fully grasp the point of this dialogue. They might say, "I told you what I need. Just build it. Haven't you ever heard that the customer is always right? Call me when you're done." This attitude undermines the collaborative approach that is the best strategy for truly understanding a problem and then determining how best to solve it.

Technical support is another domain where "The customer is always right" can get turned on its head. When people call technical support, they're already frustrated and confused because something isn't working. Many technical support conversations just make callers more frustrated and confused. Perhaps technical support people have been trained to disregard the customer's input because it's inaccurate so much of the time. That is, their philosophy may be "The customer is probably wrong." I've heard of people calling technical support because they couldn't find the "Any" key on the keyboard when the onscreen prompt said to "Press any key." Another customer complained that the computer's cupholder was broken. Cupholder? Oh, you mean the CD/DVD drive. A colleague once told me that the tech support people in his company created a special problem report category labeled "user brain damage." Clearly, the customer is not always right when it comes to technical problems with computers or other electronic devices.

Once in a while I've been delighted with customer service that went above and beyond the minimum. Here's a recent example. I wanted to get gutter guards installed on some of the gutters around my house that frequently get plugged with tree leaves and pine needles. I researched several products and contacted two vendors to come out and give me estimates. The first vendor looked at my gutters and gave me a price quote for doing precisely what I asked for: installing his screening product on certain areas of the gutters. This vendor assumed that I, the customer, was right, and he gave me exactly what I requested.

The second vendor impressed me more. He looked at the gutters I wanted to have screened and recommended a particular product as the best solution. Next, he looked at the roof areas around those gutters and identified three problems I had not been aware of: broken roof tiles, signs of leakage, and rotted wood. Then this vendor looked at several other areas of my gutters that I hadn't asked about having screened. He pointed out that they were full of debris and recommended the gutters be cleaned out. I felt like I was getting a good solution to my real problems, not just the superficial "Sure, I can sell you those" response I heard from the first vendor. I mailed the contract to the second vendor.

Here's a case where the customer (that would be me) wasn't right. My car's brakes weren't working as well as they should. I took the car to a muffler and brake shop near my house and asked them to replace the front brakes. I even had a coupon. When I picked up the car, the mechanic told me, "Your brakes don't need to be replaced. I adjusted them, and they're working fine now. No charge." Guess where I took my cars for service for all the remaining years I lived in that city? Rather than assuming that my analysis, as a non-automotive expert, was correct, the mechanic found the underlying issue and solved the real problem. This experience gave me confidence in the company's work and in their integrity.

I have a long history of writing customer complaint letters when I encounter defective products or services. A friend once called these "Dr. Karl Wiegers expects results" letters. Most of the time, my complaint is justified and I can back it up with facts and evidence. But not always. I once found some foreign material in a jar of peanut butter. I mailed the offending material to the peanut butter manufacturer with my request for a refund. Analysis showed that the foreign material was grape jam. The peanut butter manufacturer pointed out, "As we do not make grape jam, it is likely that this was introduced into the peanut butter by a knife that had grape jam on it." Oops. Sorry, my mistake. I try to keep this experience in mind when I'm unhappy with a product or service. It's important to make sure that my facts are straight, my expectations are reasonable, and this is not a case of user brain damage on my part.

The next time you're involved on either side of a customer-supplier discussion, keep the lesson of this chapter in mind: the customer is not always right, but the customer always has a point. As a customer, you're entitled to have the supplier take your complaint or request seriously. You should expect the supplier to ask whatever questions are necessary to make sure she fully understands your needs or the source of your unhappiness. As a supplier, show respect for the emotion or information the customer is providing to you, and don't be shy about following up with questions to really understand the situation. It's an application of that excellent principle from Stephen Covey's fine book, *The 7 Habits of Highly Effective People*: "Seek first to understand, then to be understood."* Through a process of respectful collaboration, a customer and a supplier usually can reach a mutually satisfactory conclusion.

---

* Stephen R. Covey, *The 7 Habits of Highly Effective People* (New York: Free Press, 2004).

Chapter 32

THERE'S PLENTY OF CREDIT TO GO AROUND

Pearl #32: Credit for work well done is something you give and share with others, not something you take for yourself.

*T*he achievements of an apprentice scientist such as a graduate student or research assistant are closely tied to the lead scientist's name and reputation. A few scientists are quite particular about taking credit for any work performed in their laboratories, regardless of which pair of hands actually did the work. Although other contributors may be given a nod in the acknowledgments, listing the lead scientist's name as the sole author of a paper does a disservice to others who contributed to the research effort.

When I was a graduate student in chemistry, I began writing papers about some of my research work. I always placed the name of my thesis advisor, Professor Stanley Smith, as the first author and myself as the coauthor. The first change Stan made in each of my manuscripts was to switch the order of the authors' names so that my name came first. I learned a valuable lesson from this: there's plenty of credit to go around.

My advisor was already well respected in the scientific community. Stan knew that I was just starting out and recognized that I had done most of the work, so he put my name first to ensure that I would get most of the credit. Thus, other chemists would later refer to the "Wiegers and Smith" paper, not the "Smith and Wiegers" paper. This was a small gesture on the part of the lead scientist, but it meant a lot to me. It also made me appreciate the importance of being thoughtful about who gets credit for a given piece of work.

This isn't just true of scientific research, of course. Throughout life, you participate in collaborative activities with many different people. In some of these situations, you do the bulk of the work, and you're rightly entitled to credit for that. In other cases, you might be a minor contributor or perhaps just a reviewer or an advisor. Regardless of your position of authority, consider passing along a good chunk of the credit to your collaborators. This causes no harm to an already-established reputation, and it increases the visibility of the other people who toiled on the project. It's also a good idea to refer to the work "we" did, unless you're describing something that you undertook by yourself.

I'm surprised when authors fail to acknowledge others who have contributed to the effort or even to the thought process that led to a book or article. In the technical books I write, I always include many references to previous publications. In part, these references give my reader additional sources of information on particular topics. Including references also acknowledges earlier authors whose work influenced my own. It's rare for a single individual to create a whole new field of endeavor, a new piece of knowledge, or a new product entirely without input from anyone else. Sir Isaac Newton, a true intellectual giant himself, said, "If I have seen further, it is by standing on the shoulders of giants." All of us get ideas from other people and synthesize those with our own understanding, which sometimes advances knowledge and progress in a particular domain.

Unfortunately, some people feel that to get ahead in their world they need to take all the credit. Sometimes they even actively diminish the work of others. When I see a technical book that contains no references, I wonder if the author is claiming to have invented everything in the book entirely on his own. Of course, he didn't. It's easy to grant credit to others for shared achievements. Put multiple names on the paper or presentation, list contributors and acknowledgments, use the word "we" when discussing the project, or name the team members and coaches who contributed to the victory.

I learned long ago that there are two ways to look good in what you do. One way is to genuinely excel. The other is to lower the baseline so that your achievements stand out more distinctly from those of others. Some individuals seem to believe that they look better in the eyes of their colleagues or audience if they can make a competitor or predecessor look bad. They attempt to take credit rather than to share credit. This can fool people who might not know the background or the other contributors in the field; however, it creates resentment among those who are in the know. It makes the offender look selfish and petty, not brilliant and creative. The superstar forward didn't win the championship soccer game alone; she had a lot of help from the other players on the field. Even if the driver gets credit for winning the NASCAR race, he couldn't have done it without massive contributions from the crew chief, owner, car and engine builders, spotters, and pit crew.

I have a friend who wrote the seminal book in a particular technical area. He is highly respected and often is invited to participate in workshops in that domain. Some years after his book came out, two other people who are also highly regarded in that area published their own book. Since then, they have sought to diminish my friend's influence in the arena and have tried to take the lion's share of recognition based on their own contributions. But credit is something you earn, not something you take. You earn credit based on the value of what you contribute to a particular field. Although these two other people have extended the basic work in an important new direction, it's unprofessional—and unkind—to downplay the foundational work that my friend performed. There's room in the credit column for all three contributors.

Unless you're working or playing in such a highly charged environment that you feel you must claw your way to the top over the backs of your competitors, there's plenty of credit to go around. Make sure that people who contribute to the achievement receive their fair share of the rewards and accolades ... and maybe even a little more than their fair share.

Chapter 33

THE LEADERS OF THE BAND

Pearl #33: Contrasting the leadership styles of two high school band directors demonstrates the importance of respect, creativity, challenge, and encouragement in motivating any organization to achieve a culture of excellence.

When I was a child, I had but two life ambitions. First, I wanted to learn to play the trumpet, possibly even becoming a professional musician. Second, I wanted to become a tail gunner in a B-52 Stratofortress jet bomber. That's what happens when you grow up on Air Force bases. Before I was nine years old, I could distinguish a B-52 from the smaller B-47 just by looking at their tails. I never did get to be the tail gunner in a B-52, but I did become a trumpet player. The experiences I had playing trumpet under two different band directors in high school taught me a lot about leadership.

I began tootling my horn in sixth grade. By the time I entered high school, band and orchestra were my favorite subjects. That first year I was lucky to have an exemplary band director, who I'll call Mr. Mellon. Mr. Mellon was much loved and highly respected. He had guided our marching band for years, and it was the best high school band in southwestern Idaho. I loved marching in the parades and performing in the halftime shows at football games. During my first year, our high school again won the championship sweepstakes award with a top rating at the annual marching band competition, beating our cross-town rival. I was proud to wear my marching uniform.

Alas, Mr. Mellon moved on to another school the following year. Replacing him was a man I'll call Mr. Houghton, who was promoted from one of the junior high schools in Boise. Mr. Houghton did considerable damage to our high school band. He might have known his music, but he wasn't skilled at motivating, inspiring, or leading a 125-member band to a stellar performance.

This comparison between two band directors—extraordinary and disappointing—provides some interesting insights about leadership. What made Mr. Mellon so successful and so loved and Mr. Houghton so mediocre and so disliked? There were several factors.

Mr. Mellon was a kind and gentle man. He knew how to encourage and coax the best performance out of his students. He was a superb teacher. He passed out compliments, provided helpful guidance to his students, and valued each band member's musicianship.

In contrast, Mr. Houghton strived to achieve results through intimidation. Instead of smiling and coaxing, he glowered and snarled. Mr. Houghton demanded a certain performance without regard for the capabilities and limitations of either the students or their instruments. Perhaps this technique worked in junior high school, but it just engendered resentment in high school students. Leaders know how to motivate the members of their organizations to achieve more than they thought they could and to be happy in the process. Tyrants simply demand results. Mr. Mellon was a leader; Mr. Houghton was a tyrant.

Mr. Mellon was a brilliantly creative musician and bandleader. He designed innovative marching formations that were interesting and challenging to execute. The band members rose to the occasion, taking pride in their ability to perform more complex maneuvers and play more sophisticated music than most bands undertook.

Mr. Houghton did not creatively challenge his students or himself. While our band was playing intriguing music that Mr. Mellon had arranged for us, nearly every other high school band was playing a popular but mundane song called "Georgy Girl." When Mr. Houghton took over the next year, my friends and I desperately hoped that we would not have to play "Georgy Girl." Sure enough, that was Mr. Houghton's idea of a good tune to add to our repertoire. Creative leaders encourage a high level of performance. They inspire and instill pride in the team members by pulling them toward great achievements. Ordinary leaders do ordinary things and frustrate those team members who know they have more potential. Mr. Mellon was creative; Mr. Houghton was ordinary.

Mr. Mellon treated all of his students with courtesy and respect, but Mr. Houghton played favorites and belittled his students. Mr. Houghton was nice to me, however reluctantly. I was the first-chair trumpet player, an important position in a marching band. He kept exhorting me to play louder during performances, and I blasted my little heart out until I literally gasped for air. It was discouraging, therefore, to receive accusatory glares from Mr. Houghton and the other band members when a judge criticized our competition performance by saying, "Trumpets and tubas were over-blowing." Hey, I was only doing what my teacher told me to do.

Many members of the band became disillusioned and dispirited after a few months under Mr. Houghton. We missed Mr. Mellon, and Mr. Houghton knew it. Anytime he would hear us "noodling" on some of the fun songs we had played the previous year, Mr. Houghton would command us to knock it off. Admittedly, we played the old tunes partly to get his goat, but mainly we played them because they brought back memories of better times in the band. Mr. Houghton didn't seem curious about why we wanted to go back a year in time. An insightful leader recognizes that he is not the font of all knowledge. Having experienced people share their experience and pass it on to newer people is one way to build a culture of excellence. It should be encouraged, not discouraged because of the new leader's personal feelings.

At that year's marching band competition, we lost both our school-size division and the sweepstakes award to—you guessed it—our archrival across town. Tears streamed down the cheeks of some of my bandmates when we heard the announcement. It didn't have to be that way. Mr. Houghton had a solid cast of musicians to work with. He could have achieved fine results had he not alienated the students through his unpleasant demeanor and uncreative leadership. My two closest friends and I didn't even take band during our senior year because we just couldn't deal with Mr. Houghton anymore.

It's tough to step into a position made vacant by the departure of a superb and beloved leader. Comparisons are inevitable. If you're ever in such a situation, take the time to understand what made your predecessor so successful. Don't try to become a clone, but don't throw away the qualities that have made the group great to date either. Capitalize on the assets of your successful and experienced team.

You'll get the best results by respecting the culture and history of the organization while looking for creative ways to take the next step and lead your team members to an even higher level of achievement. Try to be like Mr. Mellon, who molded players into a team and then steered the team to its maximum performance. Leaders like Mr. Houghton just spoil the experience for everyone.

Chapter 34

TRUST YOUR OWN WORK

Pearl #34: With experience and maturity, you acquire confidence in your abilities and learn to trust the work you do, provided that you also respect your limitations.

$\mathcal{W}$hile in graduate school in organic chemistry, I was studying a particular type of chemical reaction.* I had done one set of experiments, and my thesis advisor and I thought we understood how that reaction worked. I performed a second set of experiments using a similar chemical compound. To my consternation, the results from this compound didn't quite match my earlier results. I was talking with Stan one evening in his office. "I don't understand," I said sadly. "I thought I did these experiments right, but the curve I calculated based on the first compound just doesn't quite fit the new data. I must have made some mistake I'm not aware of."

Apparently Stan had more confidence in my experimental technique than I did. He replied, "You will get to the point where you believe your

---

* Lithium aluminum hydride reductions of ketones, in case you wondered.

results *because* you did the experiment, not *in spite of the fact* that you did the experiment."

I found this to be a powerful message. I was still early in my studies to become a research scientist, and I hadn't yet developed much confidence in my work. My advisor's response to my dismay showed that he believed I was doing the experiments carefully and correctly. The fact that my interpretation of the data didn't quite fit the experimental results suggested that perhaps our understanding of the reaction was incomplete, not that my data was bad.

Stan was right. As we continued our studies, we found that the reaction was more complicated than we had initially thought. Because I was indeed doing careful experiments, we were able to believe the data and reach a better understanding of how the reaction worked. Had I not learned to trust my results, I might have repeated the second set of experiments over and over, trying to find out what was going wrong, when in fact there was nothing wrong at all.

My scientific career was brief because about six years after I completed my PhD in organic chemistry, I changed careers and became a software engineer. My achievements as a research chemist were correspondingly limited. But I did have one shining success that reinforced the concept of having confidence in my own results.

Stan and I published two papers in chemistry journals based on my thesis research. Shortly after our first paper came out, I read a paper by another research group working on a related aspect of the same chemical reaction. Based on my understanding of that reaction, I believed I knew what was happening in the other group's experiments. I wrote to the lead scientist and sent him a copy of our paper. In my letter, I made three predictions about what I expected would happen if that group were to perform its experiments on the same chemical I had been studying. I was happy when that scientist replied, asking me to send him a sample of that chemical so he could perform the experiments I'd suggested. Collaboration is fun.

A year later I saw another paper published by that same research group. All three of my predictions came true! My theory about how this chemical reaction worked allowed me to make predictions that an independent scientist could confirm. This is the essence of the scientific process, pooling results and ideas to better understand how some aspect of the universe operates. This experience gave me more confidence in my own scientific ability. It also underscored the value of people with different backgrounds and perspectives putting their heads together to solve a problem.

Years later I relearned the lesson to trust my own work. My first book, *Creating a Software Engineering Culture*, was published in 1996. As with all of my books, I invited a number of friends and professional colleagues to review the manuscript as I was writing it. One day I received some feedback from one reviewer suggesting I make a certain change. The change seemed reasonable, so I modified the manuscript accordingly. Shortly thereafter, a second reviewer proposed that I make a change that was the opposite of the first reviewer's suggestion. Hmmm. That also seemed reasonable. I rewrote that section of the manuscript to satisfy the second reviewer. This happened a few times, and I found myself chasing the reviewer comments in a fruitless attempt to make every potential reader happy.

I soon realized that was a fool's game. I decided to write the book *I* wanted to write, not the book someone else might have written in my place. I certainly did—always have, always will—study every reviewer comment, and I take them all seriously. My manuscript reviewers and editors have provided tremendously valuable input over the years. Ultimately, though, it is my book and I need to write it to the best of my ability to say just what I want to say. After writing seven books now,

I feel pretty confident in my ability to tell the stories I wish to tell. You might like them or you might not, but they're my stories.

Sometimes, as I'm looking over a section I wrote, a little voice will nag at me. It says, "That part doesn't work; redo it or cut it out." I used to reply to myself, "Let's see how the reviewers feel about it." The reviewers invariably hated that section and suggested I change it. Hence, I've learned to trust that little voice and to fix the issue right away. The voice hasn't been wrong yet.

Do you trust your own work, whether in the lab, at the office, or around the house? Do you have confidence—but not cockiness—in your own abilities? It's a good idea to know your limits so you can get expert help when necessary and avoid painting yourself into a corner, perhaps literally.

There are some things I'm good at and many I am not. Whenever I need to do some work with wood or electricity, I turn to my buddy Norm, who is a master at both. We both have complete confidence in his knowledge and abilities. I can look over Norm's shoulder as we work on projects together to learn from his expertise. I feel a lot safer flipping the power switch on if Norm has helped me than if I had done it all by myself.

Think about what you're good at and how you can share that knowledge with others, perhaps as a mentor. Trust your own work, but don't be afraid to ask for assistance from other people when they're more adept at some activity than you are. We all do better with a little help from our friends.

Chapter 35

KNOWLEDGE IS NOT ZERO-SUM

Pearl #35: People who are stingy about sharing their knowledge with their colleagues don't understand that we all come out ahead when people pool what they know.

ike many graduate students, I was a teaching assistant for several years. I liked being a TA because I enjoy teaching and, at that time, I thought I was headed for an academic career. Unfortunately, we graduate teaching assistants received limited training in how to be effective instructors and classroom leaders. After a brief orientation, we were unleashed on unsuspecting students and did the best we could. I quickly learned that the love of sharing knowledge lies at the core of every skillful teacher.

My first teaching assignment was supervising one section of an organic chemistry laboratory course. This lab contained three groups of students with different TAs for a four-hour session once a week. I began each lab session with a short overview for my students about the purpose of the experiment and suggestions for how to spend their time effectively. Few other TAs took the time to point their students in the right direction in this way. Students from the other lab sections began drifting over to my orientations because they found them helpful.

Periodically the students in this course would have an exam. To help prepare my students, I held an evening review session before each exam. A few students from the other course sections began dropping in on these review sessions too. At first, I resented their presence and tried to kick them out; after all, the purpose of the review session was to prepare *my* students to do better on the exam. But the interlopers didn't leave.

One evening after such a review session, I was talking to my advisor, Stan, and an advanced graduate student, Ruth, back at my research lab. I related this story to them and complained about the other students sticking their noses in when they weren't invited. Stan and Ruth smiled. Ruth said, "If they want to come, let them come. Take it as a compliment about your teaching." Stan added, "There's plenty of knowledge to go around."

Of course they were right. The point of education is to teach whomever wishes to learn. In the competitive environment of a major university, particularly in a required course for premed students, it's up to the students themselves to do the best job they're able to do. My job as an instructor is simply to present knowledge in the most effective way I can to anyone who is receptive to that knowledge.

Ever since I heard that wisdom from Stan and Ruth, I've tried to be open about sharing my knowledge, whether in a classroom or other settings in my life. When I worked at Kodak, I was always happy to share anything I knew with my colleagues. I hoped they would do the same for me. After all, we were all on the same side. We had the common objective of making our company and its projects succeed so we could keep our jobs and earn money.

The key message here is that knowledge is not zero-sum. That is, I'm not losing any of my knowledge by passing it along to others. We're not dividing up a knowledge pie of fixed size. And when we pool what we know, we all come out ahead. Everybody wins.

Naturally, as a professional trainer, I need to earn a living, so I charge fees for corporate and government training engagements. When I started Process Impact, I adopted the policy that I would never do corporate training work for free. If I'm providing value to a company, I'm entitled to be compensated for that value. However, I also have a policy of never charging a fee to speak at nonprofit organizations of software professionals who are enhancing their knowledge and skills on their own time. Such organizations include professional societies, quality organizations, and process improvement interest groups. In a way, speaking for free at such meetings is marketing for my professional services. But in another way, it's simply making a contribution to the betterment of the software industry and some of its more motivated practitioners.

I've met a number of people over the years who carefully protect their knowledge. They take the concept that "knowledge is power" to an extreme. They believe that retaining a proprietary hold on what they know gives them power and control over others as well as job security.

I remember one such fellow, a software developer I'll call Roy. Anytime I asked Roy a question, I could almost see the gears grinding in his brain. He seemed to be thinking, "If I give Karl the complete answer to his question, he'll know as much as I do. That's a threat to me, so therefore I'll only give him half the answer." If I came back for more, Roy would give me half of the remaining answer to the question, so I would never get a complete answer. How irritating! Roy was a fellow employee, so I didn't appreciate his secretiveness. It was clearly a power move to dole out information in small increments to make sure that Roy always knew more about a particular topic than anyone else did.

If you're a manager, recognize that such knowledge conservers may be a liability to your organization. Should that individual ever leave your team or your company, who could pick up the ball and carry on the necessary work? Perhaps no one. Capable, knowledgeable, and experienced individuals certainly should be respected and compensated for their contributions and their value to the company. But those few individuals who insist that there's only so much knowledge to go around and who are hanging onto theirs pose an unnecessary risk. You might be better off without them.

How freely do you share what you know with the people around you? Do you and your co-workers exchange tips and techniques so you all can work together better? Does your employer appreciate the people who share what they know, or are the knowledge hoarders more highly valued? Set an example among your peers by being open with your knowledge. Gain advantage by effectively applying what you know to the work you do—and not just by possessing information. Look for opportunities to stimulate information sharing and ongoing learning in your workplace. Some of my workgroups have held informal brown-bag lunch sessions during which team members discuss articles or books they read or pass along ideas they picked up from a training class or conference presentation. There are many ways to improve the effectiveness, efficiency, and culture of the entire team.

Mentoring is an excellent way to share your knowledge and wisdom (which aren't the same things). Perhaps you know a junior colleague at work who would benefit from your coaching. Maybe you can help children learn to read at a neighborhood school. Various civic organizations exist to match up mentors with adolescents who could use good adult role models and friends.

I wish I'd had a mentor when I began my career as a consultant, trainer, and author. I had many questions. For the most part, I stumbled through as best I could, and fortunately it worked out well for me. As a consequence, though, I'm always happy to share what I've learned about consulting, speaking, courseware development, and book-writing with other software professionals who are getting started in those areas. They do not pose a threat to me, so why not help them out? Ultimately, we'll all be better off.

Chapter 36

WE'RE ALL ON THE SAME SIDE HERE

Pearl #36: People working toward a common purpose should recognize that we'll all get better results if we collaborate effectively to achieve our mutual goals.

It became fashionable in corporate America some years ago to hold team-building workshops. A variety of such activities were concocted, and numerous companies and consultants sprang into existence to fulfill every corporation's team-building needs. You could send people to the woods for a "ropes course." Or you could make a bigger investment and send your teams on challenging outdoor expeditions. For a more modest investment, you could bring in consultants who would structure a day or two of team-building activities. These events were often held as off-site retreats to get people out of their normal work context and daily pressures.

The objective of team building is to forge stronger bonds among your team members so they can work more effectively toward their common goals. The activities are intended to improve performance by helping team members get to know each other better, build trust, take sensible risks, and combine their skills to solve problems. The idea is that the insights the team members gain in this artificial environment will transfer to the workplace. It's a worthy goal. What manager doesn't want to improve the way his or her people work together? It can be valuable to understand your fellow employees: what motivates them, what's important to them, and their hot-button issues.

Kodak got sucked in by this fad, and every once in a while I was invited to participate in one of those kinds of activities. "Invited" is perhaps too gentle; "asked" is more accurate. But I hated these so-called team-building activities and participated in them only with great reluctance. I sometimes opted out of certain activities because I found them to be a waste of time and an insult to the participants' intelligence. The exercises seemed contrived, and the facilitators often didn't know enough about the participants to make the sessions pertinent. I'm in favor of good teamwork, and I've worked on a number of teams that performed very well. I just never saw the relevance of most structured team-building activities.

For example, in one "ropes course" activity, several participants bodily pick up another participant and pass her through a hole in a net made of ropes so she can be safely handed off to a group of people on the other side of the hole. I think this is supposed to engender trust in your coworkers in some way. I imagine this can happen in certain emergency situations. If you're the one stranded in your car in a flash flood, you'll have no problem trusting the rescuers on the other end of the rope, whether or not you've ever taken a team-building course. Now, I've been around for a while, but I have never seen a situation in which a bunch of office workers had to manhandle another person through, around, over, with, or between a bunch of ropes. The trust metaphor just didn't do much for me.

The great insight I gained from team-building activities was that, for some participants, this really *was* an eye-opening experience. I remember one such activity that involved about twenty-five people—experienced, adult, professional employees. During the debriefing afterward, one participant excitedly shared a powerful message he gained from the experience: "Now I realize that we really are on the same side, and we have to work together to accomplish our goals." I'm glad he came to this realization, but why did it take a contrived team-building event to make that lightbulb go on in his head? I thought we all knew that already. Apparently, I was wrong.

I did actively participate in one exercise that was intended to accomplish some team building and generate some insights. Six of us were involved, all first-line managers. This exercise involved a rectangular grid of squares laid out on the floor with masking tape. The facilitator had devised a secret pathway through that grid from start to finish that involved stepping in certain squares in a specific sequence. The goal was for all of us to make it through the invisible pathway from beginning to end with no mistakes. If you ever stepped in the wrong square, you had to start over. The wrinkle was that we couldn't speak during the exercise. This was supposed to be a metaphor for getting a product to market. Or something.

The participants came up with a plan. Each person was responsible for knowing the sequence of steps in a specific row. Each row owner was to silently guide the other players through that portion of the sequence by pointing at the next square in the sequence.

It was a reasonable plan, but it didn't go well. The participants made a lot of errors, they failed to properly guide the others through the rows for which they were responsible, and we took an inordinate length of time to complete the exercise. One woman made it all the way through and then sat down. She'd forgotten that she still had a responsibility to direct the remaining players through "her" row. (This was consistent with her personality, as she was something of an irascible lone wolf.) I found the exercise a total waste of time.

I don't know why it comes as a surprise to people to learn that collaboration, communication, respecting and trusting your teammates, and accepting and fulfilling responsibilities are important success factors for any organization. Do we really need artificial team-building exercises to figure this out?

Don't get me wrong. I believe teamwork is extremely important and that it's critical for people to learn how to work together. I've worked with some teams that "jelled" and ran very effectively. I've also worked with groups of people that were declared to be "teams" but which never acted like one. Both groups that I have in mind as prime examples included four smart, experienced research scientists. The team that jelled had precise goals, clear responsibilities, and roles for the work we did together. We pooled our results, and it took contributions from all of us to solve the problems. As it happened, we were able to achieve our prime goal very quickly. Then the interesting scientific research really began, and we figured out how a fairly complex photographic process worked. That team was a lot of fun.

The second team consisted of three people with strong egos, each of whom went his own direction, plus a highly experienced senior scientist who was supposed to be a mentor but who actually contributed very little. We sat together, but we never worked toward a common purpose. We did accomplish some useful things on our own or working in pairs, but senior management was disappointed in the overall outcome. The experience wasn't rewarding for me either.

People do need to learn how to collaborate. If you're going to be a member of a group activity, it's worth spending some time early on discussing exactly how you're all going to work together. People often skip that step, to their detriment. They assume that everyone knows how to work together, but that just isn't true. We also tend to assume that other people will think and behave similarly to the way we do.

During a retrospective at the end of one project, I learned that the members of two groups that had collaborated on the project had different communication style preferences. One group felt they had been kept out of the loop on certain issues. The leader of the second group protested. "I copied all of you on every e-mail I sent," she said. "What's the problem?" The members of the second group were accustomed to sharing information and resolving issues primarily through e-mail. However, the other group preferred face-to-face meetings to receive updates and make decisions. The two groups had never discussed these preferences during the project itself, which led to frustration and hard feelings. It's best to work out these kinds of collaboration ground rules very early in the project.

I recently worked for a short time with the board of a nonprofit organization. Two of the other volunteers with that organization didn't share my understanding of teamwork. They had collected a list of contact names for possible fundraising purposes. At the request of the nonprofit's president, I corrected a few minor errors and reformatted the data in their list so we could generate customized solicitation letters. I explained my changes thoroughly and respectfully. However, the two other volunteers interpreted my modifications as a personal assault on the value of their work. They sent an extremely nasty e-mail to me and to the president.

Frankly, I was stunned. I thought we were all on the same side, working toward a common goal of providing services to needy people through this nonprofit. I saw my activity as simply taking the next step, building on their contributions. That's how progress gets made, through collaboration and synergy. Unfortunately, those other volunteers misinterpreted my actions as a rejection of their work and an attempt by me to usurp their credit. Credit wasn't important to me at all; I was just trying to meet the president's needs. These two volunteers forgot that we had a shared purpose and objective. I don't need that kind of aggravation and disrespect, so I dropped out of the volunteer effort for that nonprofit.

After working at a company with more than one hundred thousand employees for eighteen years, I started a one-person company, Process Impact. Self-employment has suited me well, mainly because I don't like being managed and I don't like being a manager. I do enjoy working with other people toward common goals, though, and that has been one of the shortcomings of being on my own. I miss scribbling on a whiteboard and kicking ideas around with clear-thinking colleagues or getting quick feedback on an idea or on something I've written. I miss the synergy—and the stimulation—of putting our heads together to solve a problem and coming out with something better than any of us would have devised on our own.

I have learned some interesting things while being self-employed. I found that, even in a one-person company, management is unreasonable and uninformed, and the employees are all lazy with bad attitudes. Our team-building exercises, like our holiday parties, are very quiet. On the positive side, I always win the Employee of the Month award and get to park in the special parking space. Our company slogan is: "Our Employee Is Our Greatest Asset." And we really mean that.

Chapter 37

OUTSIDE THE BOX

Pearl #37: When old ways of working or patterns of behavior are no longer effective, you might need a radical change—a paradigm shift—to solve problems more effectively.

hinking outside the box. Making a paradigm shift. Looking at the problem in a brand-new way. Taking a fresh approach. These expressions all refer to changing the way we look at the world to solve a difficult problem in a better fashion. Human beings naturally get stuck in their established ways of thinking. It's all we know at any given time. But sometimes that doesn't get the job done. Instead of pursuing the current path that doesn't seem to lead anywhere, we need to break the mold and shake up our thinking, sometimes in a radical fashion.

I saw some great examples of paradigm shifts in graduate school. My thesis advisor was particularly adept at approaching problems with a fresh perspective. Our research group used an electronic interface box with numerous dials and switches on the front panel to collect data from the experiments we were doing and transfer it to a computer for analysis. One day Stan asked my lab partner and I to consider what capabilities a next-generation interface box should have. We carefully drew a diagram of a new front panel with even more switches and dials having a broader range of options. We gave Stan our diagram. He said, "Okay," and smiled his little knowing smile.

A few months later, Stan showed us the new interface box. It had absolutely nothing on the front panel! No dials, no knobs, no switches, no meters—just bare metal. The machine was controlled by software in the computer. Instead of the limited options we could build into the hardware with knobs and switches, the new box had a nearly limitless range of capabilities. This was a classic paradigm shift in thinking: moving from the design restrictions of hardware into the vast flexibility that software control provides. It had never dawned on me to change the interface box in such a profound fashion.

Experiences like this demonstrate the narrowness of thought to which even intelligent and educated people are subject. We are both enabled and constrained by our knowledge, experience, and personal creativity. Sometimes we need an outside perspective to suggest a radically different way of doing something. The trick is to cultivate the self-awareness that a novel approach might be needed to explore truly unique strategies.

Sometimes a paradigm shift jumps right out at you, as in "necessity is the mother of invention." When I was ready to leave the University of Illinois and find a job in the chemical industry, I had to have some interviews on campus with recruiters from potential employers. Historically, students had signed up for the interviews they wanted in what amounted to a race. Early one autumn morning, all the recruiters would sit at tables in a gymnasium and the students would line up outside. When the doors opened, you would race to the table for the company you were most interested in and sign up for an interview time slot. Then you'd run to the end of the line for your second-favorite company, and so on, until the recruiters had no more slots available. The strategy to ensure that you got an interview with your preferred company was thus to line up very early in the morning.

This seemed ridiculous to me. I didn't think the next forty years of my career should be determined by how early in the morning I was willing to get up on one particular day. So I proposed a new approach.

With the cooperation of a receptive placement office manager, I wrote a software application for interview scheduling. Students could use this program to specify the companies with which they wanted to interview and indicate their priority preferences. The program used a lottery approach to assign students to their first-priority companies, then to their second-priority companies, and so on. If you didn't get an interview at your first-choice company because they ran out of time slots, you went to the head of the line for your second choice.

This lottery strategy seemed fairer, and it resulted in less frustration among the people who were scrambling for jobs. The chemistry placement office used this program for years. Plus, it worked out well for me. I had a personal motivation to look for a better way than racing from line to line early in the morning.

I had a similar experience in my subsequent career as a software engineer. In 1986, I took a course called Structured Analysis and Design. The premise of the course was that there is great value in drawing certain kinds of diagrams—called models—of proposed software systems before you actually start writing the programs. To me this was a novel concept, the idea that I could represent information about a software program in some way other than writing the code itself. I immediately incorporated modeling into my software development work.

As my software career evolved, I found myself concentrating in the area of software requirements. Every project has requirements (the capabilities and characteristics of the product you're building), whether it's a small Web site, a space station, or anything in between. I quickly discovered that modeling is a powerful tool when exploring requirements. Drawing pictures is a great way to communicate, to supplement—but not replace—the natural-language text that people ordinarily use to record the requirements for a software project.

In my experience, though, few software requirements analysts practice modeling on a routine basis. It seems to be too radical a paradigm shift for many of them to adopt comfortably. They persist in simply writing a list of requirements statements in English, which are plagued by the ambiguity and redundancy that characterize all natural-language communication. When I'm delivering a training class on requirements, I'm always delighted to see lightbulbs go on in students' eyes when they realize how helpful modeling would be on their projects as a supplement to the textual requirements statements.

Incremental approaches to doing better work can get the job done in many situations. Try to do whatever you do better than you did it before, and explore a modest extension to your current body of knowledge. But also look for opportunities to radically change your basic approach, to solve an otherwise intractable problem your current strategies can't handle. You might need to find a colleague with whom you can kick ideas around. One of you might say, "Here's a wild idea. What if we tried ..." The suggestion might sound absurd at first. But it just might solve your problem in a better way.

The notion of a paradigm shift doesn't just apply in the workplace. Perhaps you and your family are trapped in some old practices or negative behaviors. Maybe the whole crowd has convened at the shore for vacation during the first week of August for decades. But as the years go by, family members become less enthusiastic about coming.

Family customs and rituals are fun and comfortable, but there's a fine line between a ritual and a rut. It's a big planet; perhaps the family would like to check out some other part of it next year. Breaking out of a historical mold usually stretches peoples' comfort level, but that can be an eye-opening, enriching experience. Look for opportunities to visit some new area, try some novel experience, or eat something you wouldn't ordinarily touch.

Or perhaps the same conflicts arise among family members over and over. Can you identify and address the root causes of the conflict? Can you decide to just turn over a new leaf and forget about past offenses and look to the future? Maybe some new ideas about relationships, responsibilities, and problem-solving strategies would be helpful. When old ways of thinking don't work for you anymore, try something new. You might like the results.

ABOUT THE AUTHOR

After growing up on air force bases around the world, Karl Wiegers landed in Boise, Idaho, at age eleven. He received a BS in chemistry from Boise State College and MS and PhD degrees in organic chemistry from the University of Illinois. Karl spent eighteen years at Eastman Kodak Company in Rochester, New York, where he worked as a photographic research scientist, software developer, software manager, software quality engineer, and software process improvement leader. In 1997, he launched Process Impact, a software process consulting and training company based in Portland, Oregon.

Karl's professional interests include requirements engineering, project management, risk management, quality improvement, and process improvement. Karl is the author of six popular books on software development and management, including the bestselling *Software Requirements*, as well as 175 articles on computing, chemistry, and military history. He has delivered more than five hundred keynotes, presentations, and training classes worldwide.

When he's not at the keyboard, Karl enjoys wine tasting, reading about military history and science, writing and recording music, playing his Les Paul and Stratocaster guitars (loudly), and riding his Suzuki motorcycle (quietly). Karl lives in Happy Valley, Oregon, with his wife, Chris. Visit Karlwiegers.com for more information.

A keen observer of daily life, Karl realized how everyday encounters can impart significant life lessons—if you're paying attention. His recollection of many such "pearls of wisdom" that emerged from conversations and experiences in his own life led him to write *Pearls from Sand: How Small Encounters Lead to Powerful Lessons.* Karl's hope is that you will find many of these lessons to be relevant to your own life, and that you'll reflect on the life lessons—your own pearls—that help you live a happier and more fulfilling life.

Join the
PEARLS *from* SAND Community

You've just read many stories about how I learned some essential life lessons. The world wants to hear your stories, too! Everyone accumulates a collection of life lessons. Here's a chance for you to share your own pearls of wisdom and to learn more from other people.

Visit **Pearlsfromsand.com** to participate in the *Pearls from Sand* community. Click on "Join the Discussion" to see the blog, where new pearls of wisdom will appear periodically. Click on "Submit a Pearl" to share your own life lessons. Selected reader submissions will be posted on the blog so we can all learn from each other's experiences.

Free Audio Book

As a special gift, you may download a FREE audio book version of *Pearls from Sand: How Small Encounters Lead to Powerful Lessons.* Just follow these steps:

1. Navigate to the Products page at Pearlsfromsand.com/products.html.

2. Choose the audio book version you want from the options shown (MP3 or Apple format).

3. Click on the Add to Cart button for that product.

4. Enter the following discount code when the shopping cart window appears: **37PEARLS**.

5. Click on the Update Cart button and the full price of the audio book will be subtracted from the total price of the items in your cart.

You'll receive downloading instructions when
you have completed the transaction.

BUY A SHARE OF THE FUTURE IN YOUR COMMUNITY

These certificates make great holiday, graduation and birthday gifts that can be personalized with the recipient's name. The cost of one S.H.A.R.E. or one square foot is $54.17. The personalized certificate is suitable for framing and will state the number of shares purchased and the amount of each share, as well as the recipient's name. The home that you participate in "building" will last for many years and will continue to grow in value.

Here is a sample SHARE certificate:

THIS CERTIFIES THAT

YOUR NAME HERE

HAS INVESTED IN A HOME FOR A DESERVING FAMILY

1985-2010

TWENTY-FIVE YEARS OF BUILDING FUTURES
IN OUR COMMUNITY ONE HOME AT A TIME

1200 SQUARE FOOT HOUSE @ $65,000 = $54.17 PER SQUARE FOOT
This certificate represents a tax deductible donation. It has no cash value.

YES, I WOULD LIKE TO HELP!

I support the work that Habitat for Humanity does and I want to be part of the excitement! As a donor, I will receive periodic updates on your construction activities but, more importantly, I know my gift will help a family in our community realize the dream of homeownership. **I would like to SHARE in your efforts against substandard housing in my community!** *(Please print below)*

PLEASE SEND ME _____ SHARES at $54.17 EACH = $ $_____

In Honor Of: _____

Occasion: (Circle One)   *HOLIDAY   BIRTHDAY   ANNIVERSARY*

  OTHER: _____

Address of Recipient: _____

Gift From: _____ *Donor Address:* _____

Donor Email: _____

I AM ENCLOSING A CHECK FOR $ $_____ PAYABLE TO HABITAT FOR HUMANITY <u>OR</u> PLEASE CHARGE MY VISA OR MASTERCARD *(CIRCLE ONE)*

Card Number _____ Expiration Date: _____

Name as it appears on Credit Card _____ Charge Amount $ _____

Signature _____

Billing Address _____

Telephone # Day _____ Eve _____

PLEASE NOTE: Your contribution is tax-deductible to the fullest extent allowed by law.
Habitat for Humanity • P.O. Box 1443 • Newport News, VA 23601 • 757-596-5553
www.HelpHabitatforHumanity.org